The Resolute Outsider

The Resolute Outsider

Overcoming odds ➡ *Achieving ends*

Elizabeth A Fagan AKC, MSc, MD

IBSN-13: 9798413527573

Cover design by David L Smith

Printed in the United States of America

Book Reviews

'The Resolute Outsider by Dr Elizabeth Fagan is a story about drive, determination and resoluteness when pursuing dreams despite external challenges. She speaks honestly about the challenges that she faced, from a young age, and continues to be vulnerable about the difficulties that followed later on in her career. As a medical student, from a lower socioeconomic background, it is beyond inspiring to see such an inspirational individual achieve all these incredible career landmarks despite having such a difficult start in life. This book has taught me about the importance of always wanting more for yourself and continuing to strive for a better future despite current circumstances.' BARBARA FALANA, FINAL YEAR MBBS STUDENT, KING'S COLLEGE LONDON.

'Elizabeth showed grit and determination to make her mark on her profession. Her story will help others at the start of their journey to believe in their own potential.' ALEXANDRA CHAPMAN, SENIOR DEVELOPMENT MANAGER – INTERNATIONAL FUNDRAISING & SUPPORTER DEVELOPMENT, KING'S COLLEGE LONDON & KING'S HEALTH PARTNERS.

'Elizabeth is nothing short of an inspiration. It's wonderful that others can now be encouraged by her story.' MEGAN BRUNS, DEPUTY DIRECTOR, FUNDRAISING AND SUPPORTER DEVELOPMENT, KING'S COLLEGE LONDON.

'It is a great privilege to be able to write a few lines about the inspirational journey the author has undertaken to achieve her dream of becoming a doctor whilst overcoming social, domestic and financial disadvantages. As Elizabeth Fagan says "attending King's College London (KCL) opened doors beyond imagination given my disadvantaged background" and as co-Director of the Extended Medical Degree Programme (EMDP) at KCL I know how important it is to continue to give such opportunities to potential doctors. I am sure that students at KCL and elsewhere will benefit from reading about the barriers that she has overcome, and I know it will *resonate with them even though times have changed. I have no doubt that reading this book will help give young people the confidence to follow their dreams even if it means challenging stereotypes and overcoming barriers. Above all this book shows the value of persistence, hard work and resilience to achieve your life goals. It is an inspirational and uplifting read.'* PROFESSOR STEVE THOMPSON, PROFESSOR OF IMMUNOLOGY, EDUCATION & WIDENING PARTICIPATION AND CO-DIRECTOR OF THE EXTENDED MEDICAL DEGREE PROGRAMME, KING'S COLLEGE

Acknowledgements

This is a work of non-fiction. Some names have been changed to preserve anonymity.

This book comprises a series of essays formulated over years and prompted by friends, family and contacts who urged me to chronicle my life's story. The aim is to encourage readers, especially students and others starting out, to be resolute in overcoming life's challenges.

To my friends and teachers who supported me when 'the chips were down', I say a humble thank you. I remain in your debt. In return, you gained in me a friend for life and in all weathers. I gravitate towards people who have experienced, and overcome, hard times.

To our mother, you sacrificed happiness and dreams to give your daughters an education – the key to opening the door to opportunities you never had.

To those who encouraged me and went the extra mile, I draw comfort sharing the same Earth.

Attending King's College London (KCL) opened doors beyond imagination given my disadvantaged background. I give thanks for the support and encouragement offered over many years when these necessities were not widely available in my era. At KCL, and other forward-looking institutions of learning, the moral and financial support offered to disadvantaged students warms my heart. I applaud the concerted outreach by the College to lessen inequity and inequality.

To those who could, even should, have been there, I believe you lost an opportunity to enrich your own lives by helping someone when she was down, but not out. You missed not being there to see her rise once more.

To anyone considered an outsider, I say, embrace, rather than shy away from, your differences. Treasure your exceptions. Many outsiders make a positive impact. There is room for all of us.

Permission from the British Medical Journal granted with thanks to reprint in part (Chapter 14): A patient who changed my life. *British Medical Journal 1993; 307: 1330*

Abbreviations and Acronyms

ADH	Anti-diuretic hormone; regulates fluid balance. Produced in the brain, regulated by the pituitary gland
A-levels	University entrance examinations in the UK for high-school pupils typically taken at ages 16-18 years
Bart's	St. Bartholomew's Hospital and Medical School in East London
BMA	British Medical Association
Board Certification, USA	Certification following examination by the American Board of Medical Specialties (ABMS) after completion of Internship (equivalent to HP) and Residency (similar to SHO/Registrar) and denotes specialisation e.g. gastroenterologist
BS	Batchelor of Surgery; typically awarded with MB after 5-6 years undergraduate study at medical school
BSc	Batchelor of Science
Co-Ed	School or institution accepting male and female pupils/students with mixed gender classes
CT	Computerised Tomography scan
CV	Curriculum Vitae: Resumé summarising training and achievements
CWAC	Canadian Women's Army Corp (1942-

	1946); eventually merged into the Canadian Army
ECFMG	Educational Commission for Foreign Medical Graduates; entry level examination to practice medicine in USA
ECG	Electrocardiogram
E-11	E-11 visa: An independent visa with Green Card (Alien Resident) qualification to live and work in the USA
Eleven-Plus: 11+	A 'transfer' test taken by 11-12 year olds in most of the UK until 1976 to determine subsequent state-funded secondary education; grammar school, secondary modern ('Comprehensive') or technical school
Enosis	Movement by armed mostly Greek Cypriot fighters (EOKA) to end British Colonial rule and unify Cyprus with Greece
ENT	Ear, nose and throat
EOKA	Εθνική Οργάνωσις Κυπρίων Αγωνιστών (Ethniki Organosis Kyprion Agniston); Greek guerrilla organisation in Cyprus fighting for end of Colonial Rule, self-determination and union with Greece
EMDP	Extended Medical Degree Programme at KCL; provides some financial support for disadvantaged medical students
FACP	Fellow of the American College of Physicians
FRCP	Fellow of the Royal College of Physicians; granted to MRCP holders with outstanding achievements
FRCPath	Fellow of the Royal College of Pathologists; granted to MRCPath holders with outstanding achievements, including research
Fulminant	Abbreviation for Fulminant Hepatic Failure, also termed Acute Liver Failure.

GBV-C	A pegivirus (formerly known as hepatitis G virus) that infects humans but is not known to cause disease
GMC	General Medical Council; Governing body for Registration of doctors in the UK
H-1	H-1B visa; granted typically through a sponsoring employer in the USA to allow a foreign person with speciality training temporary permission to work
HCV	Hepatitis C virus
HIPAA	Health Insurance Portability and Accountability Act (1996)
HP	House Physician; typical 6-month post in first year after qualification as a doctor in the UK
HS	House Surgeon; typical 6-month post in first year after qualification as a doctor in the UK
IDPR	Illinois Department of Professional Regulation; grants medical licences for physicians and surgeons (036) to practice in Illinois, USA
JCHMT	Joint Committee on Higher Medical Training (UK); organised by the Federation of the Royal Colleges of Physicians (UK) that oversaw general (internal) medicine and speciality training - similar to Board Speciality training in the USA. Taken over by the Joint Royal Colleges of Physicians Training Board (JRCPTB).
KCHMS	King's College Hospital Medical School
KCL	King's College London; the largest college within London University
KOL	Key opinion leader
LCH	London Chest Hospital, Bonner Road, East London; closed in 2015

LSE	London School of Economics
LSU	La Sainte Union; Convent high-school in Bath, England; amalgamated with Cardinal Newman Comprehensive School in 1979
MB	Medicinae Baccalaureus (Batchelor of Medicine); typically divided into 2nd MB, after approximately 18 months and later 3rd and 4th MB, for qualification
MD (UK)	In UK, a postgraduate degree based on research and doctoral thesis; MD in the US is the qualification (graduation) degree of a medical doctor
MGH	Massachusetts General Hospital, USA
MRC	Medical Research Council
MRCP	Member(ship) of the Royal College of Physicians
MRCP Parts I, II	Postgraduate examinations in General Medicine, similar to 'Boards in Internal Medicine' in USA
MRCPath	Member of the Royal College of Pathologists
MRI	Magnetic Resonance Imaging
MRT	Mass Rapid Transit
MSc	Master of Science
NAAFI	Navy, Army and Airforce Institutes: A British military company established to provide goods and services
NATO	North Atlantic Treaty Organisation
PRCP	President of the Royal College of Physicians
RAOC	Royal Army Ordnance Corps; branch of the British Army that supplies goods and ammunition
RCP	Royal College of Physicians

RFHSM	Royal Free Hospital School of Medicine; part of London University
RPMS	Royal Postgraduate Medical School; An independent medical school linked to Hammersmith Hospital, London. Merged with Imperial College School of Medicine in 1997
RUH	Royal United Hospitals, Bath, UK
RUSH	Rush Presbyterian St. Luke's Medical Center and University, Chicago, Illinois, USA
SAS	Specialist and Associate Specialist doctors
SHO	Senior House Officer: Post beyond first year after qualification (MB, BS) as a doctor; similar to 'Fellow' in the USA
Sixth form	Years 12 and 13 (Ages 16-17); Lower and upper sixth. La Sainte Union Convent required an extra year (14) for Physics at A level
S-level	Scholarship-level (optional) examination at high school; typically taken by pupils likely to obtain an A grade at A level
SPEX	Special Purpose Examination: Illinois Department of Professional Regulation (IDPR) typically set for established physicians exempt from Board/s certification
statim	Latin term used in medicine for 'without delay'
TMT	Türk Mukavemet Teşkilatı: Turkish Resistance organisation to Cyprus uprisings
UCCA	Universities Central Council of Admissions (1961-1993); now UCAS - a clearing system for University entrance
UNESCO	United Nations Educational, Scientific and Cultural Organisation
Wellcome Trust	A charitable organisation funding medical research and based in London, UK

Introduction

As a white, tall, English and educated person born in the UK many may not suspect, even comprehend, the challenges, biases and prejudices someone like me faced from childhood into young adulthood.

As a family, we lived a double life. On the surface, my sister Mary and I, the progeny of two soldiers who fought in World War II, experienced an exotic life full of adventures as we travelled and lived abroad in several countries. Underneath this veneer, life was tough for our working-class family. Daily living and education (for me, ages 5-12 years) became disrupted, especially when we lived in conflict zones within Cyprus (1958-1962). Our parents were miserably unhappy in their marriage. We concealed for years the domestic abuse emanating from our father, a career soldier proud and determined to keep untarnished his military record.

Many viewed as unreachable my life-long ambition to become a doctor. The deck for progress seemed stacked against me. We viewed England, the land of my birth, as foreign on return from abroad in 1962. I faced my 12th birthday lacking basic knowledge and skills that peers took for granted. Scraping through to high school (school year 9, aged 13 years) teachers at first relegated me to the bottom of the bottom class when medical schools required top grades at A level for university entrance, especially for women. As a teenager, I lived under the constant threat our father would pull me out of school. He saw no value in higher education. In contrast, our mother, also uneducated, viewed learning as the key to escape our 'prison without bars'. Several obstacles threatened to derail my aspirations and career. Mother and I became homeless and penniless, albeit not 'out on the street', amid my A level examinations. I was left to solve and resolve a Sword of Damocles I kept secret for years.

This book highlights the need to be resolute and determined to overcome obstacles that straddle the cobbled path of life. The kindness and encouragement of teachers, friends and strangers need to be acknowledged. The support of any parent who sacrifices personal happiness for a child's future should be honoured. Lessons can be learned about swallowing pride and asking for help when 'the chips are down.'

There are advantages to being an outsider. There is room for all of us. We should treasure our exceptions.

Table of Contents

Chapter 1: So, you want to be a doctor?

'One does not ask of one who suffers: What is your country and what is your religion? One merely says: You suffer, that is enough for me. You belong to me, and I shall help you.' Louis Pasteur (1822-1895).

There is no obvious explanation for my wanting to be a doctor. I chose this path before I could read or write. I do not come from a medical family. No 'Aha!' moment came either from watching television and movies or seeing the family doctor in action. I watched without envy as several school peers yearned to be actresses, dancers or some high-profile luminary. My future profession chose me, absent starry eyes. 'Saving lives' was too lofty a goal. I wanted to care for the sick, for better or worse.

At home during my primary (junior) school years, we rarely discussed these aspirations. I was awkward, clumsy and slow to master the three 'Rs' – reading, 'riting, 'rithmetic - despite an eagerness to learn. My sister, Mary, older by two years and much more in maturity, easily conquered these milestones. Our parents, both army veterans of World War II, focused on the day-to-day challenges of military life. We lived and breathed the British army's way of life. In father's view, women ran the household and raised the children. He provided the money for essentials only, thereby completing his household obligations. For mother, her war-time experiences and harsh upbringing in western Canada translated into tough love. As an army wife, separated from her country, relatives and living abroad in various countries, she raised us alone.

The British military moved around frequently in the 1950s and 1960s. Military families, often referred to in deployment orders as 'baggage', always seemed one step behind and in tow. We moved out to join father in Singapore (1954-1957) via Beirut, Bahrain and India followed by

Cyprus during the island's Emergency (1958-1962). We lived day-to-day. Immediate issues overrode educational needs. Where do we live? When do we move again?

The inevitability of changing schools and missing classes became par for the course as an army brat. Until I became a teenager, the family's attitude towards schooling was 'catch it when you can'. Any school would do, local or military. School was school, no questions asked. We joined a new school often in the middle of a term, in the middle of a week. More than once, mother removed us from school during a class lesson. We were on the move again, sometimes to a different country and with no advanced warning. Saying goodbye to friends became the norm. Mary shed endless tears over friends and pets never to be seen again. I stopped making friends as the easier option to cope with our peripatetic lifestyle. The luxury of connecting instantaneously via social media, emails and all things Wi-Fi would take several more decades. Blue aerogram letters, restricted to three small pages, offered a lifeline – a long one with weeks to turn around. We moved too often for any continuity of addresses. The military post office system gave a low priority to civilian mail. We spent several birthdays packing up, sitting on boxes in near-empty army quarters. Key belongings, shipped out weeks ahead to the next destination, left us with only the clothes on our back and a small bag of essentials. No toys. During the most troubled times in Cyprus in 1958-1959, (Chapter 3. 'Blood on my shoes') we moved four times in nine weeks.

Consequently, a tipping point came in 1961 as I was soon to turn 11, and Mary 13, years of age. I could write out individual letters of the alphabet but not cursive-style writing. A critical point in my education loomed: the dreaded '11-Plus' examination. Pupils in the UK typically took this exam between ages 11-13 years. A pass grade opened doors to high school (years 9-13) and the opportunity to sit A-level exams for university entrance in the final two years. For highly competitive medical school, and especially for women as a distinct minority, top grades in the final A-levels were essential in biology, chemistry and, especially, physics. Lesser grades would not secure an interview, let alone a coveted place. Pupils who failed the 11-Plus were relegated to a comprehensive, rather than grammar, school. In the 1960s, most comprehensive schools offered only the GCSE - the General Certificate of Secondary Education

– at that time considered inferior for university entrance and certainly substandard for medical school.

Mother decided to bring Mary and me back to the UK to improve our education. Mary passed the 11-plus examination in Cyprus and should have started in a grammar high school. We viewed England, the country of our birth, as foreign on our return to the UK in 1962. We faced an alien civilian lifestyle. Our teenage years coincided with the swinging sixties except we did not swing. Social class distinctions were prominent in the UK. Mother chose La Sainte Union Convent, an independent high school for girls in the city of Bath in the West of England. This school favoured elite and upper-class families, not us solidly working class. The school took day pupils and borders. Importantly, the school waived tuition fees for the first child of the family to attend if, like Mary, she passed the 11-Plus examination.

What a change from our usual casual schooling! Nine lessons per day. Hours of homework. A reprimand would follow not wearing the obligatory white gloves outside the school gates. The boater summer hat had to be worn flat on the head with brim parallel to the ground. On any second offence, one could be expelled from school. As a religious order originating in France, we addressed the nuns as 'Madame', albeit pronounced the English way, 'Madum', rather than 'Sister', one of the many incongruities of the school. Most of the nuns were Irish or English.

Mary, approaching 14 years of age in 1962, became the 'all-rounder' and made the leap early on to blend in at high school and beyond. Our trajectories diverged.

The nuns placed me, almost 12-years-old without the 11-Plus examination successfully in the rear mirror, into the Preparatory (junior) school in another part of the city. They considered me 'too far behind' (polite term for 'backward') to sit the 11-Plus examination the same year; however, the clock was ticking. For a year, the teachers sought to increase the chances of my passing this all-important hurdle, interspersing regular lessons of the three 'Rs' with customised, multiple-choice test questions tailored to the level of 'that exam'. Fundamentals other pupils took for granted had to be learned. I counted currency in Cypriot Lira (pound), 50 mils (a shilling) and piastres (pence), not their British equivalents. Britain only changed to decimal currency in 1971 and Cyprus changed to the Euro in 2008. Abroad, we counted numbers in

Turkish; 'Bir, iki, üç' – one, two, three – and modern Greek; 'Ena, thio, tria'. Fractions and multiple division tables were foreign to me.

On an early summer's day in 1963 and soon to face my 13th birthday, the nuns announced the date of the 11-Plus examination. Time was up once I became a teenager the ensuing September. The day of the examination came without fanfare. In a nondescript classroom devoid of wall decorations, I joined a small group of pupils from our school armed with a blunt pencil and booklet. An outside adjudicator started the clock: You may begin.

First question: Write a brief description of an English country garden. You have thirty minutes.

Gosh! So, there are special gardens in English out in the countryside?

My mind turned to our time abroad. The imagination and logic of a child blossomed as I struggled to complete the answer: *Hmm... I will write about orchids. These grow along the roadsides in Singapore and must be part of the English countryside and garden because they are common.*

As children in Singapore, we visited frequently the Botanic Gardens - our local park, replete with freely roaming monkeys and numerous plants considered exotic in the West but not to a child unaware of typical flora in the UK. Thus, I continued to describe flowers from Singapore, albeit only by colour and smell, based on the logic: 'They must be English flowers because an Englishman (Sir Stamford Raffles) founded the Gardens.' Only as an adult I learned that the Gardens initially were modelled after Kew Gardens in West London. In 2015 the Singapore Botanic Gardens became a UNESCO World Heritage site, recognised worldwide for the unique, exotic flora. Before moving on to the second exam question, I added roses and 'snapdragons' for good measure based on vague recollections of our year in Buckinghamshire.

Second question: Write about what you enjoyed at a football match. You have fifteen minutes.

'A football match?' I remembered how music heralded large sporting events among soldiers in the army. I recall writing about brass bands as in a military tattoo. I covered my uncertain tracks by adding: 'and then, I woke up. I was dreaming.'

Now to the multiple-choice section: What is the opposite of Youth? I had never heard of Maiden.

No one at home mentioned the exam. Life revolved around daily preparations for school.

The 11-Plus results came in. I did not fail. I did not pass either. My marks were exactly in no-man's land. At that time, the nuns did not reveal these borderline results: 'You have won an interview.'

I replied cheerfully: 'Oh, good. I will be with my big sister.' Silently, I added: 'Great, I won. I must have passed easily.'

I assumed the interview would be a simple formality to enter an elite grammar high school. That no-one else in my class faced one, made me feel special. Ignorance can be bliss. As a 12.5-year-old and naïve I believed my future aspirations were good enough. After all, I am going to become a doctor when I grow up. Now I can tell someone important outside of the school.

School and home life continued as usual without preparation or coaching for the interview. When the day came, the concern at home focused on navigating transport outside my usual travel route. Will I be in time for school lunch?

After two bus rides and a walk, satchel in hand, I entered the gates of a school in Wiltshire, the county where we lived. An administrator directed me into an oak-panelled study to be interviewed by the principal of the school. After witnessing years of drills and parades in the army, strict discipline at home and at the convent school, the formality of the occasion did not bother me. These were the days when children from my background curtsied before authority.

I was surprised the principal was male – and short. Since we entered civilian life on returning to the UK, we rarely interacted with males. Home was all females as was school. We joked that only female garden plants grew within the convent walls. Our father, away most of the time, kept his distance during brief visits.

The principal wore a brown corduroy jacket and tie. He radiated a no-nonsense approach. No problem for an army brat.

He looked up at me: 'How old are you – again?' I towered over him at 5 feet 11 inches (180 cms).

'I am nearly 13 - in September.' An age with '-teen' attached seemed much more grown up than 12 and a half.

He seemed puzzled, flipping through my records: 'Please sit down. So, what do you want to be when you grow up?'

Now was my chance: 'I want to read medicine at London University. I want to be a doctor.'

He seemed surprised: 'Hmm.' He leaned back in his chair, now poised on two legs - an infringement at my school. My body language befitted that of an awkward, shy schoolchild and betrayed this bravado statement, clearly rehearsed.

'So, you want to be a doctor?' His tone implied 'Are you sure?'

'Yes, yes, that is what I have wanted my whole life.'

His whimsical smile must have reflected the brief period representing 'my whole life.'

'Well, what happens if you fail to get into medical school? You know it's extremely competitive to get there.'

'I will not fail. I will get there.'

'Yes, but even the best pupils fail to get into medical school. What will you do if you fail?'

'I will try again.'

'There are many other jobs to aim for. Have you thought of any others?'

'No, I want to be a doctor, I will get there... I will make it, I will.'

Another 'Hmm' before he continued: 'You seem very determined, despite.......' He paused, closed his files, stood up promptly and nodded: 'Well, anyway, I wish you good luck.'

A buzzer sounded. The same administrator entered: 'You may go now.'

I curtsied to the surprise of both adults. The administrator escorted me out.

The interview, to decide which fork in the long road of educational achievement would open or close, lasted less than ten minutes. Before I could gather any thoughts, the administrator pointed to the bus stop nearby. A bus would take me into Bath, an hour's journey and a walk across a field to join my class at the junior convent school. Just another day spent catching up again.

I came away with little insight into how the interview went and no understanding of the enormous implications for my future. All along I assumed this interview was a 'win', a formality for any child determined to become a doctor.

'So, how was the interview?' I simply shrugged my shoulders nonchalantly when approached by the nuns.

School and home life continued uneventfully. The choir needed alto-range singers. I filled a slot at the back row behind the majority chorus of sopranos. The preparatory school choir performed well. We won first place at various local and regional choral competitions.

Several weeks later, the nuns told me without ceremony that I passed the interview. Mother would be informed by letter. They made no mention of a place in their grammar high school. Again, I assumed a free place would follow automatically to join my sister in the big school.

Mother seemed anxious after receiving the letter. Our parents argued in a separate room. In those early days, they made some attempt to keep disagreements out of earshot. Thus, I learned that my acceptance into the convent high school required fees as was typical for more than one child attending per family. The alternative local comprehensive school required none; however, pupils usually left without the requisite examinations necessary for university entrance.

Money remained tight in the household. Our family had no financial safety net. The convent grammar high school offered a discount to military families. Regardless, the discounted sum represented more than 20 per cent of our family allowance. The army provided a flat-rate weekly pay in vouchers to support the spouse and children with no extras for added expenses, let alone school fees. Over the years, the army allowance remained the same regardless of the needs of a growing family, inflation and rising school fees. Moreover, both parents viewed paying for education an alien concept. Both left school before 15 years of age. Father saw no merit in a high-school education for anyone let alone girls. He considered he had done well without such a luxury. Accordingly, we lived under his constant threat of my being pulled out of school despite mother carrying the burden of finding money for school fees. Mother wished for us to have the best education possible but could not see a way to paying. Fully aware of her limited opportunities in life through a lack of education, she recognized my steely determination to do well. She began to plan on how to squeeze out the fees from within an already tight household budget. Mother kept her priority to feed and clothe us - typical teenagers with large appetites and growing out of clothes and shoes at an alarming rate.

The nuns found us 'hand-me-down' clothes after girls had left the school. An ill-fitting blazer and overcoat miraculously were resewn into good fits. The signature school hat, the boater, had to be a custom fit for me at added expense. The school recommended several sets of summer and winter outfits, sportswear, and indoor and outdoor shoes. We could only afford one set of any clothing. We were taller than the teachers. Our summer school uniform dresses – one each and extra-long, had to be custom-made of material from the original school-clothing manufacturers. Shoe sizes exceeded the maximum provided by the school-approved footwear company. Comparable shoes required an extensive search before approval by the nuns.

Maintaining our school uniforms became a consuming ritual for mother. Every day on returning home around 6.00PM we deposited our two summer dresses or winter shirts into the bathtub before supper. Mother washed these by hand. Uniforms hung by the coal fire in the kitchen, the warmest room in the house, or on the outside washing line, depending on the weather. Without fail, by 6.00AM each school morning, all clothes were dried and ironed ready to wear for that day, come rain or shine.

Mother took on part-time work as a nurses' help and cleaner (domestic) at two local hospitals. In those days, a domestic cleaned floors and bedpans and made beds. She became an essential but faceless worker for the rest of her working life.

The excitement at starting high school quickly faded when the nuns placed me in the back of the classroom in the bottom of the bottom class - the lowest (class 'W') stream among pupils least likely than 'Y' and 'X' streams to qualify for university entrance. One step forward, many back. My sister and I missed out twice. Living in an army bubble while abroad we had limited opportunities to immerse ourselves in the rich, diverse cultures, local languages and histories. Back in the UK, and land of our birth, we were foreigners again, this time to the British way of life, to English history, customs and traditions.

Despite these handicaps, the biology teacher, Madame Ignatius Maria, recognized my determination and motivation to do well. I approached her several times after class to ask for science lessons rather than needlework and crafts. She cast the deciding vote propelling me up to the 'fast' (X) stream during the second term in 1964: 'Unfortunately, you have lost out on a term of work in the sciences, and we are well into the syllabus....'

'I am used to starting at page 173.' Some advantages come from a military family – being accustomed to catching-up.

As Catholics we aligned with father's staunch Irish background of frequent attendance at Mass, singing in the choir and being an altar 'boy'. Of necessity in 1947, mother converted from her Russo (Eastern) Orthodox religion to the Catholic faith to marry a Catholic. She became devout, albeit quietly. Faith formed her pillar as the façade of their marriage crumbled over the years.

As teenagers, Mary and I participated in our Confirmation ceremony held at St. John's Catholic church in the city centre of Bath. In the 1960's, this ceremony in the Catholic church typically took place as a teenager. Unlike Baptism held soon after birth, Confirmation represents a voluntary acceptance of continuation within the Catholic faith. The nuns approved summer school uniforms as appropriate dress for our height rather than age. Many other candidates wore the traditional gossamer white dresses and veils.

After the ceremony, I remained in church in a back pew on my knees in prayer. The ceremony invoked the seven tenets of the Holy Spirit. My prayers sought at least three - wisdom, knowledge and understanding – to enlighten physics lessons.

The head girl at the time, Jocelyn Corrigan, walked up from behind. She dressed well, spoke eloquently and radiated poise and confidence. Her father was the mayor of the city – we lived worlds apart. Jocelyn tapped me on the shoulder. I rose, a custom for any pupil to stand in the company of the head girl.

'So, I hear you want to be a doctor?' Her tone was inquisitive. My long-standing aspirations across the school were well known. Jocelyn wished to study medicine too. As head girl and a clever, multitalented person, she was well on her way.

'Yes, and I am going to apply to London university, to Bart's (St. Bartholomew's) and King's College.' I learned only a decade later, that King's had been her first choice.

Her puzzled expression betrayed her composure. Her response shattered mine. She exclaimed: 'But.... you can't read Medicine....you're working class!'

And with that, Jocelyn turned on her fashionable heels, head held high and walked away. Fortunately, she exited too promptly to hear me sigh 'Oh, no,' and witness my tears. I sank back onto the pew, head held low and covered my face with my hands to hide from passers-by. Our parents raised us to respect authority, not to answer back, not to challenge an opinion coming from anyone senior regardless of doubt in its substance. Bullying can take on many forms - not that I recognised this behaviour at the time. In my mind, as the most senior pupil in the school, the head girl had the gravitas to make such a proclamation. Many in the school, including me, viewed her as the perfect pupil -- multi-talented in the arts and sciences. Moreover, she dressed elegantly outside of school and spoke confidently in public with perfect diction. Importantly to me, she certainly would gain a coveted place at medical school in an era when few were open to women. Now I had two black marks against me – being female and working class. Little did I know that our paths would cross once more, albeit fifty years later (Chapter 17. 'Didn't we do well?!').

Years later and two-thirds near my goal with top (A) grades in A-level chemistry and biology under my belt, the nuns revealed the headmaster's written assessment regarding the 11-Plus examination: 'I give her the benefit of the doubt - a pass grade …. she seems determined to be a doctor; however, given her disadvantages in background and education so far, I doubt she will succeed in her ambition…but wish her well.'

Chapter 2: A double life

On outward appearance, our family displayed the positive attributes embraced by the military - strength, resilience, harmony as one. This outside veneer bore little resemblance to the inner turmoil and dysfunction at home. Our family lived a double life.

The contrast between our lives at home, outside and abroad are stark when considering our parents' background and heritage. Our mother, the youngest of eight children, was born and raised in western Canada. Her parents, immigrant peasant farmers from Ukraine, received land by the Canadian government in return for settling near Edmonton, Alberta at the turn of the 20th Century. Family members spoke Ukrainian at home and typically married fellow Ukrainians in their local ethnic Eastern Orthodox church. Many are buried in the adjacent Kysylew (*Kyseliv*) cemetery named after their hometown in Bukovina, a region controlled by the Austro-Hungarian Empire when our grandparents lived there. This region became part of Ukraine in 1991 after declaring independence from Russia.

Mother's family experienced hardship. Her father, our grandfather, died within two weeks of her birth. Two older brothers left home shortly afterwards (1917-1918) to fight abroad at the height of World War I. Siblings raised each other. Survival meant farming through harsh winters lasting months. The family relied on food grown on the farm and stored excess produce in the frozen ground for later consumption. School consisted of a one-room classroom more than a mile away. Children walked there without shoes regardless of the weather and terrain. None had an opportunity for education beyond 13 years (eighth grade). Boys went into farming. Girls married early. Several of mother's sisters were married before, or soon after, her birth.

As numbers to farm the land dwindled at home, our mother dreamed of faraway places. She was tall for her generation (5 feet 7 inches; 170

cms), blond, blue-eyed, outgoing and vivacious with an eye for fashion and adventure. She spoke her mind, especially about exploring beyond the boundaries of her limited upbringing.

Our father was the youngest of five children born to staunch Irish Catholic parents near Dublin, Ireland. He too was tall (6 feet 2 inches; 188 cms) for his generation, lean with dark hair. He looked at you awkwardly through one eye - the other blinded in a childhood accident. We know little about his upbringing. His older sister, Elizabeth, raised him. Our first names are a coincidence, nothing more. He rarely mentioned family and background. The army dominated all thoughts and what little conversation we shared. His manner at home and work remained the same - fully moulded by the military with emphasis on discipline, rules and regulations. Children are not heard and do not cry.

On the surface, our parents shared a common thread in their histories, albeit separated by the Atlantic Ocean. Both completed only an eighth-grade education. Father's family expected him to follow in the footsteps of his father, working as a labourer on the docks near Dublin. Mother's family expected her to work on the farm or marry early as did her female siblings. Both parents bucked family traditions. Father volunteered to join the British Army as World War II threatened. His family viewed this choice as defiance since Ireland remained neutral, at least in name, during that period. He became a career soldier in the Royal Army Ordnance Corps (RAOC), worked in supplies and ammunition and supported the Normandy landings on D-Day. He continued to be deployed to unsafe and unpredictable parts of the world including for the Korean War (1950), Suez crisis and Reconstruction of Japan following World War II (1950-1952). Mother, across the Atlantic, signed up early in the War effort also as a volunteer. In 1942 she joined the recently formed Canadian Women's Army Corp (CWAC: 1941-1946) that eventually merged into the Canadian Army. Both served overseas and 'at the front' when underage. They met towards the end of World War II. Mother drove an ambulance and served as an administrator's aide in the UK, Netherlands and Germany. She remained in Europe for a year after Germany's surrender as part of the Allied Occupation in Berlin. Meanwhile, father helped evacuate prisoners from Bergen-Belsen in 1945. Their paths crossed when mother, also stationed in Germany, escorted foreign collaborators. She carried a Smith and Wesson revolver with pride and rode a motorcycle. Theirs is a typical war story. After a few brief meetings while transitioning through the UK in 1945, they exchanged addresses on the back of a packet of Camel cigarettes, followed by transatlantic blue aerogram letters after returning to Canada and Ireland, respectively. World War II was their 'finest hour' and shaped their attitudes towards everything; being resilient and independent and 'soldiering on' were unspoken tenets that permeated our lives.

After their once-in-a-lifetime experiences during the war, neither could pick up where they had left off back home. Soon after being demobbed in Canada when the CWAC era ended in 1946, mother packed her bags and headed for the UK where father was stationed. Her oldest sister, the family matriarch, waved goodbye at Winnipeg train station with the final statement: 'You are dead to me.' These words sounded the death knell for any remaining bond with her family. Our parents married in early 1947 in Dublin at St. Patrick's Cathedral. A few of father's relatives attended. That day signalled the solitary high point of their 22-year marriage.

At the time of my sister Mary's birth in November 1948 our parents lived in army quarters assigned to Bramley Ordnance Barracks, Hampshire, a euphemistic term for a single room with a hotplate stove. I followed in 1950. The UK lacked infrastructure and resources to begin repairs of the war damage and resurrect the food supply chain. Food rationing continued after the war, including for military families. Mother recounted endless queues to exchange food coupons for meagre weekly allowances of staples – bread, meat, two eggs, two strips of fatty bacon. Nothing edible went to waste. Cooks boiled animal bones for hours to eke out nourishment. Wild rabbits caught fetched a premium, as did any meat. Non-smokers traded cigarette coupons for butter, or more often, lard and margarine. Almost everyone smoked, including our parents. Senior Service cigarettes through the military (N.A.A.F.I.) store came in cartons of 500 or more.

Soon after my birth in 1950, father was posted to Korea and Japan before transferring to Singapore in 1954 where we joined him and his garrison. Singapore was recovering from the aftermath of Japanese occupation and massacres (1942-1945). These ended less than a decade before our arrival. The tragedy of the war was lost on this three-year-old.

Only decades later when in Singapore during my 1988 World Lecture Tour, did I come to appreciate the astounding resilience of the people and futuristic development of this small island nation. In the 1950s, the military used the world-famous Raffles hotel as a military club. Singapore Slings, a popular cocktail invented at Raffles, to a small child meant sailing down the bannisters to be caught by servants dressed in sparkling white uniforms with red turbans. I viewed Raffles as a playground full of exotic animal skins hanging on the walls and carpeting the floors. Colourful birds chirped away in ornamental wicker cages throughout the building.

Despite father's lowly rank as a corporal, our lives and standard-of-living changed dramatically on arrival in Singapore in 1954 after stopping with long layovers in Lebanon (Beirut), Bahrain and India (Calcutta; now Kolkata) along the way. First, we lived in the Changi district of Singapore, close to the once infamous prison that now includes Changi Airport. Later, we moved into a spacious two-bedroomed flat served by several maids, including a cook, laundryman and gardener. Maids handstitched our clothes. We dressed in local silk, hand-embroidered, rather than in cotton or 'those synthetics' considered inferior by the locals. The servants addressed mother as 'Memsahib' or 'Missy'. She was not expected to cook or care for the home, including the children. Our maid, Cinnam, took over the household with her generous size and personality. She saw her role as protector of children from the harsh realities of military life. More than once Cinnam threatened to take us 'babies home to Malaysia' after we were scolded by our parents for some infraction. The army paid for Cinnam to cook for us; however, she preferred to receive a bowl of first grade rice prioritised for army consumption.

Britain remained under war-ration conditions until 1954. In contrast, food in Singapore was plentiful, full of variety, colour and spices. Cinnam served dishes prepared by her family including durian, a large spiky tree fruit native to regions of Malaysia and other parts of Southeast Asia. We soon learned why she prepared durian away from our flat. The odour of durian, considered by some to smell like a mixture of mouldy socks, turpentine and stale onions, is sufficient for the opened fruit to be banned from several public spaces. We ate with our hands as did the Malay locals or with chopsticks. We made rice balls to mop up hot curries prepared from spices held in large banana leaves. We slurped from bowls shark's fin, and bird's nest, soups, all brimming with spices. The smells of curries, spices and fruits wafted out of houses with open windows and mixed with odours from open drains and sewers, especially during monsoon seasons.

At the docks we watched the loading and unloading of crates containing fruits unavailable in the UK – rambutans, mangoes and pineapples. Dock workers sliced fresh pineapple with an enormous, curved blade glinting in the sun, dipped a slice in salt and handed us a piece wrapped in The Straits Times, the daily newspaper. Nothing compares with the inky taste of that fresh pineapple.

Elephants, monkeys, and multi-coloured birds became part of our lives. The military assigned a female elephant to our family – our own 'Jumbo'- for us to follow her activities and well-being. Elephants played an important role in the revitalisation of Singapore following World War II. They hauled logs and heavy equipment for building construction. This educational aspect was lost on me, a naïve 5-year-old. I assumed every child had access to an elephant, much to the amazement of peers when we returned to the UK. We considered the Singapore Botanic Gardens, now a UNESCO Heritage site, to be our local park (Chapter 1. 'So, you want to be a doctor?'). Monkeys swung from tree to tree as we fed them peanuts. Orchids grew wild by the roadsides. No one bothered to pick them.

Against this exotic background, I first became aware of my surroundings. A normal routine for children in Singapore would be considered alien in the UK. We made our beds minutes before retiring to avoid sharing the night with 'creepy crawlies'. We banged the heels of our shoes on the ground before venturing a toe into them. These rituals, entrenched to avoid snakes and spiders, carried over long after returning to the UK and much to the amusement of pupils and teachers at our elite school in England. Mosquito nets draped over four-poster beds. We filled empty tin cans with water or disinfectant before placing one under each bed leg. This served to prevent, or more likely only deter, ants from climbing up. Bamboo shutters enclosed open windows without glass. Local birds flew in and out and perched on the veranda. During monsoon seasons, Cinnam, with a sixth sense for any pending storm, rushed around closing the shutters minutes before a downpour. We looked forward to thunder and lightning storms as these often heralded in a cooler period. Such storms lasted several days and nights.

Our mother, a devout Christian, eased away any fears as thunder rumbled for hours: 'Don't worry, God is just moving the furniture around in heaven.' Clearly, God must be an itinerant.

As children, we loved the monsoons – a time to run out into the rain, sometimes with a shampoo bottle to wash our waist-length hair. Runoff from the heavy rains emptied into open drains and flooded the streets.

We spent most weekends at the army recreation club; Gillman Campground (now Gillman village) with the large swimming pool as main attraction. Sirens forewarned of any threats, including pending monsoons. On one such an occasion, an open army jeep with driver and spare attendant in front whisked mother, Mary, me and my teddy bear into the back seat and headed home. Too late. Amid the torrential downpour, the jeep skidded under a large lorry carrying felled logs. Our driver was killed. Mother suffered a minor laceration requiring stitches. The hospital staff cleaned her blood off my teddy bear. I witnessed death firsthand. To explain mourning to a five-year-old, our parents took us to the funeral of a Malaysian neighbour. All attendees dressed in white. The atmosphere was one of celebration. Musicians and dancers entertained interspersed with a banquet offering platters of delicious food. The celebrations continued over several days before a procession led to the burning of the deceased person on a pyre. I came away happy to attend more funerals.

As young children, we remained blissfully unaware of any health risks from mosquitoes, rodents and other pests and tropical diseases. We were not given any malaria prophylaxis. Through the military, we received basic healthcare, mostly routine vaccinations against poliovirus, typhoid (T-A-B) and tetanus often repeated every time we moved.

'Which arm, left or right?'

'No, not the right arm, that one is full-up.'

The army provided dental check-ups. My fear of dentists remained for decades based on childhood experiences. Army dentists drilled and filled teeth under the mantra of 'children do not cry. You are in the army.'

Without access to air conditioning, now considered essential in Southeast Asia, buildings relied on large ceiling fans. These circulated in the main rooms of our flat and doubled up for drying clothes. Our father's newly washed regulation trousers spun around the ceiling as a priority. Mother's blouses had to wait. The maids took our clothes down to a river to wash. We kept a store of spare buttons to replace those smashed against rocks as part of the cleaning process.

We walked to school or travelled by rickshaw regardless of monsoons, high humidity and heat and long before the famed Singapore Mass Rapid Transport (MRT) system became operational. I started at Pasir Panjang co-educational primary school soon after my fifth birthday in September 1955. Lessons conducted in Mandarin, Malay and English reflected the ethnic origins of the pupils. Any recollections of lessons are sparse. I could not read or write. I recall only singing practice and playing games in the courtyard. Four years after arriving in Singapore, on return to the UK aged seven, I could barely read and count numbers to twenty. I struggled to complete the alphabet.

Outside of school, with only half days of lessons, life revolved around the army and military families. Interactions with the local population remained minimal. Throughout our experience as army brats in Singapore and elsewhere, we received no encouragement to learn a language other than English or to immerse ourselves in the rich local cultures, history and traditions. We lived inside a military bubble, and a small one at that.

The camp celebrated Christmas, Easter and other Western events, as if we were in the UK but without context. In December, typically the wettest and most humid month of the year in Singapore, we sang 'Good King Wenceslas' never having witnessed snow, frost, or gruel. Regardless, mother embraced local customs. Red Chinese lanterns decorated our ceilings at Christmas time and for the Chinese New Year. The nativity scene in our Catholic church portrayed all religious figures as Asian or African. For Guy Fawkes' night in November, the army built large bonfires and burned effigies of Guy as fireworks lit the starry skies. We enjoyed the spectacle without understanding the historical context of parliament and potential assassination of royalty and religious undertones.

On the outside, our stars rose with this much higher standard of living than in the UK. Our few contacts in the UK described us as exotic, with 'interesting and exciting' lives during our times abroad in the early post-war years of the 1950s to early 1960s. But our parents were miserably unhappy in their marriage. Theirs was a match made in hell with little in common except the bond forged through wartime experiences. That link soon evaporated as their generation preferred to look forward, not backward. As with many military veterans, they rarely talked about the horrors of war. Moreover, we lacked physical and emotional support from family. Mother's relatives in Canada cut her off for leaving against the family's wishes. We grew apart from our Irish relatives, having minimal contact and little in common from life's experiences.

Mother, always the extrovert and gregarious, made friends up and down the rank and file of the military. As a Canadian, she spoke outright, at first too direct for British (and Irish) tastes. Regardless, people were drawn to her 'American' accent and expressions, alien sense of humour and extra smart dress code. By contrast, our father, the die-hard soldier, all business and with no fuss, kept a low profile and practiced a best-to-keep-quiet attitude. Although proud of his heritage, he sought to blend in as an Irishman who fought alongside the British, rather than adopting the neutral stance of the Republic of Ireland during World War II.

Thus, our double life began. On the outside, nothing seemed amiss. Army life revolved around drills and parades interspersed with a social life centred around the Mess, Gillman pool and the collection of shops (N.A.A.F.I.) with military discounts on alcohol and cigarettes. Chain-smoking was the norm. Our parents, with a natural distaste for liquor, rarely drank alcohol, to the surprise of their peers. Social gatherings segregated according to rank and commission. The wives affected the ranks of their husbands and expected to be addressed as Sergeant X's wife, Major Y's wife and so on. Few wives of enlisted men crossed the divide to interact outside of formal gatherings with officers' wives. Mother became the exception. Her popularity irritated our rank-conscious father who thought she acted above her station in life.

The physical violence by father towards mother worsened as the years went by as did the verbal threats to our lives. We would be killed if we so much as hinted to anyone all was not right at home. Ammunition and a variety of guns formed an integral part of father's work and extended into our home.

We returned to England in 1957 to face another contrasting change in lifestyle. The army provided rented accommodation -- a farmhouse in Adstock, a small, typically English village in Buckinghamshire. The residents, many of whom had not ventured beyond the county boundaries, viewed us as 'that odd family from abroad'. The local food available revolved around the four seasons and harvests. That year, marrows, cabbages and apples were plentiful. Bread and potatoes became staples in place of rice and noodles. The British palate in the 1950s was bland by our tastes. Neighbours boiled green vegetables for hours and cooked meat without condiments or spices. Mother searched endlessly and unsuccessfully to find chilies to make a curry.

Schooling was equally bland. Mary and I (aged nine and seven years) attended the local one-room village school up the road. We shared the only classroom despite two years difference in age and learning levels. My underdeveloped skills in the three 'Rs' persisted. One year and one day later, we departed for Cyprus with no significant improvement or expansion in our education.

When I relate our posting to Cyprus in early 1958, without exception, people ask: 'What was the British Military thinking?' Sending a family knowingly into a recognized area of conflict is difficult to explain even decades later. The British Army believed in keeping families together regardless of the dangers and restrictions imposed.

'Why were you not sent to boarding school in the UK?' The British Government paid for schooling of military children sent home from abroad. Despite the conflicts at home as well as outside, our parents and their generation believed family should stay together through thick and thin. 'Until death do us part' included the children.

Curfews, food rations and other restrictions began within weeks of our arrival in Cyprus. The conflict, verging on civil war, between Greek- and Turkish- Cypriots -- the Cyprus Emergency, began around 1955 (Chapter 3. 'Blood on my shoes'). In 1958, the violence reached a peak and extended to civilians including military families. In October 1958, terrorists fatally shot Mrs Catherine Cutcliffe, a military spouse, while out shopping with family near Famagusta, a town on the east coast of the island. We lived nearby.

Daily life focused on survival. Regular schooling went by the wayside. Of the first three years in Cyprus, we attended classes irregularly for less than ten months. At the peak of the conflict, we moved four times in nine weeks, had our school bombed and took lessons under military guard. Bars on the windows of the school bus and at home were the norm. The parish priest carried a loaded weapon in church, marginally concealed under his robes. Soldiers attending church services genuflected with a Sten gun or Bren gun held on the left as they blessed themselves on the right. Shots fired outside the church disrupted my First Holy Communion service. Only when a tenuous and temporary peace took hold on the island after 1960 and curfew restrictions finally lifted, did our lives on the outside resemble normality by military standards. By then we had moved to Dhekelia, one of the two remaining UK sovereign bases left on the island.

Regardless of the tentative peace, the military remained ready for more conflict. During an ordinary weekend, my sister and I were at home in Dhekelia. Outside temperatures in Cyprus exceed 30°C (86°F) for most of the year. We kept doors and windows open to create a breeze. The army did not provide ceiling fans or air conditioning.

A sergeant from my father's regiment knocked on the door: 'Here are your blankets, one for each member of the household.'

With military precision, he counted out and handed over four heavy grey wool blankets each with a distinctive red border.

'Why do we need blankets?' We dressed in shorts and T-shirts as befit the Mediterranean climate especially in the summertime.

'Oh, these are your burial blankets. Look after them well as they are military property. You will need to give them back, if you leave Cyprus.' One could add 'and, only if alive.'

Meanwhile, the physical violence against mother escalated at home. She hid black eyes behind sunglasses. Bruises meant wearing long-sleeves despite the hot weather. Father was not physically violent towards Mary and me at that stage. Instead, the threats against mother escalated as we grew older and led to constant tension within the household. We always had to be on our best behaviour.

'Do not disturb dad…. he is in a bad mood (again).'

We were not *good* children – we were *saints* by some standards. Visitors commented to our parents: 'Oh, your children are so well behaved…. A delight to have.' Children of our generation were seen and not heard. No red flags warned the outsider. No one looked for red flags. Our silence and low profile as we soldiered on perpetuated the unhappiness and delayed any resolution.

Finally, in late 1961, the army notified us of our pending return to the UK. Mother worried about our education, or lack thereof, and kept pushing for our return to be accelerated. Our father's posting in Cyprus neared its end. The island had entered a relatively peaceful period. Travel around the island became less restricted. We visited spectacular historical sites, including the Salamis ruins dating as early as the 11th century BC, and began to appreciate the beauty of Cyprus. Larnaca, now occupied by an airport, was a favourite beach, deserted in our time. Despite a lessening of the conflict between ethnic factions, some limitations remained. Certain foods especially yeast and leavened bread remained a distant luxury harkening back to our year in Buckinghamshire.

We viewed England, the country of our birth, as foreign on our final return to the UK in February 1962. On arrival the army gave temporary accommodation in a camp near Berwick-upon-Tweed, a small town in northern England near the border with Scotland. That winter in the UK remains one of the coldest on record with unprecedented snowfalls and below-freezing temperatures. Snow ploughs arrived from Canada. We landed from sunny Cyprus in cotton dresses, short, ankle-length socks and without coats. The military camp consisted of a series of Nissan huts with meagre heating from a small wood-burning fire in the middle of a draughty room. The military provided four narrow camp beds, each with a single thin blanket. Our thoughts returned to those heavy grey burial blankets left behind because we had not died. None of us slept. Instead, we huddled around the central stove trying to keep warm and take turns stoking the fire.

Despite the shock of knee-deep snow and blizzards, the return to the UK offered an upside. We ventured out into the town at first light, primarily to buy winter clothing. As we rounded a corner, the smell of yeast and freshly baked bread overwhelmed us. The little corner bakery shop opened for the day. The proprietor began filling the shelves with bread, buns, rolls and all-things leavened and warm from the oven.

The portly lady turned to mother while arranging freshly baked bread loaves and rolls on a shelf: 'How can I help you?'

'I will take the lot,' was mother's immediate reply. We ploughed into the bread before exiting the shop much to the consternation of the proprietor who muttered: 'What odd people. Must be foreigners.' To this day, the smell of freshly baked bread triggers those memories.

After three years of rations in Cyprus added to our parents' war-time deprivations, we never wasted food. The day we left Northern England for the South, mother offered a neighbour excess bread buns she had bought.

The neighbour looked puzzled: 'Oh, we don't eat buns, only bread.' She remained bewildered when mother shed tears walking away saying, 'You don't understand what we have lived through.'

We moved to the West of England to Wiltshire. Mother, my sister and I entered 'civvy street', a civilian lifestyle foreign to us in our homeland, while father continued to work during the day in a nearby army camp. All through high school (1963-1969), we lived a double life at home. We attended church every Sunday, come rain, come shine, come violence in the home. As the episodes of domestic abuse escalated over the years, mother sought refuge in her adopted religion.

The final blows came in 1970 when she filed for divorce after 22 years of marriage and while sheltering in the convent of the Sisters of Charity in Bath. Father did not contest the proceedings. He did not attend. The court awarded against him on the grounds of cruelty. However, in 1970 the laws of the land favoured the husband. The Matrimonial Proceedings and Property Act of 1970 had yet to be enacted. The court made no exception as to whether leaving home was a voluntary act or occurred under threat to one's life. After all, she, not he, abandoned the home.

From that time, mother's situation spiralled downwards. The court awarded all material assets, without exception, to father despite her 'win'. On appeal, the court eventually awarded to mother a meagre allowance based on assessed needs of three pounds per week without adjustment for cost-of-living changes and inflation over the years. For us, back to second-hand clothes. For mother, back to cleaning floors and toilets. Years later, when she attempted to return to Canada, the Canadian Embassy in London denied any reinstatement of citizenship or permanent residency. Canada blacklisted her record. In 1954 she had been forced to renounce irrevocably her Canadian citizenship to take her children abroad on her passport as the wife of a British soldier. The emigration authorities made no allowance for mother's military service in World War II or for her earlier renunciation of citizenship being the only option at that time.

Over a few short years, mother surrendered several ke*
identity as was obligatory at that time. These early decis*cts *of her*
seal her unhappy fate. Relatives in Canada disowned he*lped to*
home and marrying an Irish Catholic. To marry a Catho*ving*
conversion to the Catholic religion. Her Canadian citizenship *ed*
renounced irrevocably to take her British children abroad on he*
be British) passport – no dual citizenships in those days, even for *
within the Commonwealth and no separate passports for childrer.
response of the local Catholic church to divorce took away her
anchor. The Catholic church permitted a divorcée to confess in
confessional where all sins are forgiven but for years banned her from
receiving holy communion, a core engagement for Catholics, akin to
excommunication. So much for forgiveness even for non-sinners. She
carried the shame of her divorce and the rejection by her family, country
of birth and Church all the way to her grave 35 years later.

Chapter 3: Blood on my shoes

The Island of Cyprus, basking in the Eastern Mediterranean, seems an idyllic place to raise a young family. This beautiful island offered many opportunities, especially for two rapidly growing children. We yearned for a return to the exotic lifestyle and warm climate experienced before in Singapore and after a year and one day in damp, grey England (1957-1958). My sister and I reimagined endless days of sunshine. Crystal-clear seas and white sandy beaches awaited as our playground.   We looked forward to a delicious Mediterranean diet, limitless fruits and, oh, spices again.

Not so in the 1950's. We arrived in Cyprus in early 1958 amid a major conflict between ethnically separate inhabitants – back to restrictions in travel with curfews added, disrupted schooling and food rations, again, army-style.

Our father's deployment to Cyprus between 1958-1962 coincided with the height of The Cyprus Emergency. This conflict began three years earlier (1955) when a Greek Cypriot organization (EOKA; *Εθνική Οργάνωσις Κυπρίων Αγωνιστών*, National Organization of Cypriot Fighters) mounted armed resistance to end British colonial rule and unify Cyprus with Greece (*Enosis*). The Turkish Cypriots, a minority population on the island, opposed these actions and favoured partitioning. The British military moved its Middle East headquarters from Suez to Cyprus in 1954. Stationed personnel primarily defended strategic military sites and covered military operations in the Suez Canal, Jordan, and Iraq. Not surprisingly, the British military and families became caught in the middle of the conflict between Greeks and Turks. Our father deployed to Cyprus as part of the British military surge considered necessary by the UK government to anticipate and contain the rapidly escalating conflict. This time predated division of the island along ethnic lines. In fact, enactment to partition the island into predominantly Turkish and Greek sectors occurred only years later, in

1974, after more insurgencies. Two military bases (Akrotiri and Dhekelia) remain under UK Sovereign rule.

We arrived in early 1958 amid high tensions expected to worsen. EOKA, albeit a much smaller presence than the armed forces, began targeting British military camps and installations. Their aim to create chaos and distraction drew international attention to their cause. Soon after, EOKA also escalated hostilities against Turkish Cypriots and a left-leaning element (communists) within the local Greek community. In return, the Turkish Cypriot community, mostly through a paramilitary group (TMT; *Türk Mukavemet Teşkilatı*), fought back. A war loomed between Greece and Turkey, regardless of both being allies under NATO.

The British army families lived in local villages among Turkish-Cypriots who, at that time, aligned with our military. Daily life, simple and restricted, revolved around staying safe, curfews and balancing out food rations. Strict instructions and daily drills prepared us to run, duck, and take cover in our windowless bathroom. These daily challenges overrode any priority to go to school. Life's lessons focused on survival, not the three 'Rs'. We became adept at interpreting siren signals. The 'all clear' for my sister and me, aged ten, and eight, years, signalled playtime outside but only nearby with one eye fixed on our house and one ear attuned to sirens.

When a narrow window of relative safety opened, we ran to the local corner café to collect bread. The local population and military families ate flat, unleavened bread as a staple, given the absence of yeast and unpredictable food rations. Mother, recalling her wartime experiences, maximised the amount and variety of food available. She recruited other military spouses to share a taxi to shop for food. No safety in numbers or being civilian. We learned only years later of the harrowing episodes – tyres slashed, purchases abandoned on the back seat, guns pointed at women - as ethnic opponents took their anger out on the taxi driver.

In between curfews, village life revolved around the corner café. As we weaved our way between the crowded tables to collect bread at the inside counter, Turkish Cypriots nodded in recognition. They sipped strong dark coffee, smoked pungent cigarettes and played board games.

One day, with bread in hand, we turned from the counter to go outside. Rapid shots fired. Bullets flew randomly into the café from several armed gunmen in a taxi that sped by. We knew what to do – duck, hide under the tables and run for cover at the earliest opportunity. As children, we left the mayhem behind once the locals signalled for us to run home. We ran, dropping the bread as Mary tugged at my arm to run faster.

'Oh, have you been hurt?,' mother gasped after opening the door. Our eyes followed hers looking down to see blood on my shoes.

'No. But we dropped the bread.'

Life carried on. No further discussion. A reminder in church that Sunday: 'Give us this day, our daily bread.'

Fast forward more than twenty years. As a busy doctor at the Hammersmith hospital in West London, I looked forward to a rare night off duty, and a special one at that. A good friend invited me as a guest to attend the British Academy Film Awards (BAFTA) to witness presentation of his award. I 'dressed to the nines' – a white brocade gown borrowed from my sister, hair piled high with ornate flowers and matching white satin shoes purchased for this special occasion.

In the 1970s, doctors could be called upon at any time – we did not work in shifts. My emergency pager buzzed. As the emergency back-up endoscopist that evening, I returned to the hospital urgently. An elderly and confused patient with a stomach haemorrhage required an endoscopy. No time to change clothes. I jumped into a taxi and headed for the hospital at full speed. The nursing staff assisted me to 'gown up' over the brocade gown and cover my hair. No time for pleasantries. Once gloved, I performed the endoscopy, stopped the haemorrhage by cauterising a bleeding vessel, stabilized the patient with intravenous fluids and handed him over to the regular medical staff.

I hailed another taxi for a London theatre – the Talk of the Town - feeling pleased I would arrive just in time for the awards. The theatre side-door was closed leaving open only the main entrance for celebrities. The large double doors swung open. Everyone turned around to look at the celebrity, fashionably late.

Gasps: 'Are you hurt?' The audience paid no attention to my gown, hairstyle or fashion accessories. Blood covered my shoes.

The following day, I returned to the hospital to review the patient from the previous night. He was sitting up in bed, alert and eating breakfast.

The Resolute Outsider

'How are you this morning?'

He looked at me, puzzled: 'Who are you?'

'I am your doctor, the one who ....'

His disappointment showed: 'Oh. Why can't I have the
last night? I didn't realize the doctors on night-shift were s《 *from*
— so beautiful. *ous*

Chapter 4: Rising to the top; almost there

Events in the final high school year 1968-1969 remain etched in memory half a century later. The 1960s brought rising awareness of civil rights including worldwide protests against the Vietnam war. University students in the UK and elsewhere displayed 'Ban the bomb' slogans, marched and staged sit-ins in public buildings and college campuses.

This global turmoil contrasted with the limited, sheltered and child-like life within our convent school walls. A few pupils like me, now legally adults after turning eighteen, began the third, and optional (14th) final year in the sixth form (Chapter 5. 'Beware - do not feed; this specimen is rare'). We could vote and buy alcohol; however, we remained children at school and home. Several non-cloistered orders of nuns in the UK relaxed their own dress code but not the La Sainte Union order or their pupils. Regardless of age and maturity, high school pupils wore the same uniform including ankle-length white socks when, out of school time, teenagers and adults wore nylon stockings and miniskirts. We changed outdoor, and indoor, shoes several times daily to cross between buildings. Gloves and hats remained compulsory wear outside of the school walls when in uniform.

The final autumn term began in September 1968. My daily routine over the years stayed the same except I was alone. My sister, Mary, had escaped our home situation and moved on to nursing school at St. Bartholomew's ('Barts') in London. Mother, with unfailing regimental precision, woke me promptly at 6.30AM with breakfast prepared. I dressed carefully in the school uniform, freshly washed and pressed overnight, before leaving at 7.15AM. The house had no central heating. A simple paraffin stove kept the bathroom or kitchen warm until I departed for school. After a three-quarter mile walk to the train station, a 20-minute train ride and a further half-mile walk to the convent gates, the school day began in earnest. Assembly started promptly at 9.00AM.

All pupils gathered in the main hall for communal morning prayers and to hear announcements from the headmistress and other senior staff. Although a sizeable portion of the pupils were 'non-Catholics', all joined in the religious activities regardless of faith and affiliation – no exceptions. My daily routine at school also remained unchanged – hang my coat and hat in the cloakroom and carry into class my bag, stuffed with last night's homework before entering the main hall.

The headmistress, Madame Bernard Xavier, stood outside the hall counting the pupils, noting absences and whether the school uniform complied to her standards. Madame Bernard Xavier compensated for her short stature with a generous width and billowing habit that trailed behind as she flowed silently along the hallways and stairways. No one saw her feet as she glided by. Pupils and teachers feared yet revered her. She would not take 'no' for any answer. A request meant a command. I viewed her as the top general in the army: 'Yes, Madame, absolutely, Madame.' She singled out pupils to be disciplined, not praised. Regardless, pupils tested her limits. We used nicknames: 'BX', for her and other prominent nuns including 'Madame Iggy' for Madame Ignatius Maria, the biology mistress, and more.

A few mornings into the autumn term, Madame BX beckoned while standing outside the assembly hall.

'Oh, dear, what have I done?' Other pupils gave me a wide berth and sympathetic glance, happy for the opportunity to bypass her watchful eye.

She held out the palm of her hand: 'This is for you.' The coveted red and bronze shield – 'Head Girl.'

I was stunned.

In my mind no one was less suited to that role. Senior pupils, especially prefects, staff and the governing committee typically recommended a final-year pupil for this role. I remained the ultimate outsider, resolute in mind and solitary in purpose to gain top marks (grade A) at A- level physics required for entry into medical school as a female. On that basis none would, or should, have recommended me.

A head girl in the UK at that time held a prestigious and high-profile role. Given the historical prominence of La Sainte Union Convent High School in Bath, the school carefully selected the head girl to be a role model. She projected proficiency in all aspects of school and outside.

Duties included giving speeches, attending, and representing, the school functions within the County and beyond. She typically took lead role in the annual school play. To many, Jocelyn Corrigan, the head girl two years ahead, epitomized this role. (Chapter 1. 'So, you want to be a doctor?'). She excelled in all aspects of school performance – the arts, sciences, public speaking and more. In addition, she came from a prominent family in Bath and readily 'took the stage'. Her mannerisms exuded confidence, capped by a flare for fashion and elegance. Jocelyn stood out the more in my memory because we had only one key fact in common - to become a doctor. Not surprisingly, she excelled in her A-level exams and already enrolled in medical school in Bristol.

Rather than feeling pleased and honoured, my tunnel vision saw this role as an imposition, a significant obstacle and major distraction from 'acing' the physics exam only a few months away.

I easily revealed my displeasure, shaking my head in dissent: 'No, oh no.'

More pupils scurried past in consternation on hearing the forbidden 'no' to the headmistress.

I lowered my voice to prevent further embarrassment to both of us: 'I am sorry, Madame, but I cannot take this badge.'

'But I insist.'

My anxiety about not completing the school year due to the rapidly deteriorating situation at home rose to the surface: 'No Madame, you must understand. I cannot accept this. Our home is in a bad way. We have big trouble at home.'

'I know, but we all agree you will do an excellent job.' I ignored this compliment.

In this final year, I counted down the days to see if I would, even could, complete the school year. A major roadblock loomed ahead. In mid 1969, after 25 years of distinguished service, father faced retirement exactly when I would start the final batch of A-level exams. He would be home permanently – a milestone we dreaded. Father repeatedly threatened to pull me out of school despite mother's efforts to pay the school fees and related expenses. He became physically violent towards me from my mid-teens and openly derided our value - worthless, useless, a waste of time and more.

'I am not sure I will be able to finish the school year.'

Madame BX looked at me without emotion. As was her custom, she tucked her hands, badge included, into the front folds of her habit. Her hands and feet vanished as if floating on air.

After a brief pause, she presented the badge again, took my hand and placed it firmly in my palm, shiny side up: 'This will help you to get into medical school.' The magic words.

More magic: 'As head girl, a letter of recommendation from the school will accompany any pending interviews for university medical school.'

In those days being head girl spoke volumes. She had me in the palm of her hand as mine held 'Head Girl.'

I showed no gratitude, only more concern: 'I will need help. I am not like the other girls who can do everything and get top grades in A-levels.'

'Don't you worry about your predecessors. The staff will see to that. Now run along. We must start the assembly on time. Don't tell anyone until I announce this.'

The headmistress glided into the assembly hall, her habit flowing behind as she mounted the stairs, rang the large bronze hand bell that denoted the start of assembly and began with daily prayers.

I followed behind, clutching the small badge tightly in my hand. Classmates interpreted my worried, unhappy expression as running afoul of Madame BX. Commiserations beamed silently my way. We bowed our heads in prayer.

Without fanfare, the headmistress announced: 'Elizabeth Fagan has been appointed Head Girl…. and now for other items….'

The congratulations and positive acknowledgements from my classmates surprised me. I wonder after all these years what pupils thought about my selection for such a coveted role. Head girl would have been the icing on an already rich cake for many classmates. For me, the school handed me ingredients to bake one and, hopefully, one day to add icing and candles.

Father gave no response when I showed him the badge. He preferred to water his vegetable garden. Mother viewed this accolade as a promotion in recognition of my hard work rather than hers. She was especially pleased that failure to pay on time the school fees on several occasions had not influenced my standing in the school.

On the winter uniform, I wore this badge of honour on the tie. To the yellow dress for summer uniform, prefects added a distinctive sash (girdle) of burgundy, the core school colour. Mother proudly hand-stitched the added central white stripe on the sash, denoting head prefect - head girl. All pupils stood when I entered a classroom. I rang the assembly school bell alongside the headmistress.

Shortly after my appointment, Madame BX announced her pending departure at the end of the school year after being headmistress for more than a decade (1958-1969). On the few occasions we discussed issues in the school, I saw a different side to this formidable person. She treated me with respect, radiated confidence in my abilities to balance duties with studies and gave praise when I completed a request, no longer a command. A hint of sadness came through when mentioning plans extending beyond 1969. As a nun grounded in her faith, she accepted the pending changes. What will be, will be.

True to her word, the headmistress and staff supported me, albeit in a low-key, matter-of-fact way. Protocol dictated the prefects reported to me; however, the staff oversaw their day-to-day functions to minimise my interactions. The nuns curtailed outside events declaring the school focus on the future merger with Cardinal Newman school, a task completed only a decade later. Uniform became mandatory for outside functions. The nuns abolished 'mufti days' for the final (14th) year pupils, much to the chagrin of classmates who looked forward to sporting the latest fashions. This was the swinging sixties with miniskirts, winklepicker, pointed, patent leather shoes and high stiletto heels, all the rage. Given elevation to head girl, I gladly forfeited my pending minor role as a background soldier in 'Jeanne d'Arc', the school play. The nuns typed out and helped rehearse the welcoming speech I delivered at the annual prize-giving ceremony.

Of the six applications allowed through the recently formed Universities Central Council on Admissions (UCCA) in 1968, I gained interviews at my first two choices of medical school within London University – 'Bart's, where my sister was training to be a nurse, and King's College London (KCL). Lacking confidence in obtaining even an interview in the UK, I applied independently to Trinity College, a medical school in Dublin, Ireland, not to please my disinterested Irish father but to add a seventh 'shot on goal'. Trinity offered me a place without an interview but conditional on a top grade in physics A level. Medical school seemed within reach with two top A levels under my belt – only physics left to conquer.

First up, an interview at Bart's. A senior medical student showed a small group of us candidates around the hospital and medical school. He emphasized the long and distinguished history of that teaching college dating back to 1123. The all-important interview took place in a large, empty wood-paneled room interspersed with murals. My footsteps echoed as I walked to the far end of the room. Three nondescript, expressionless people sat behind a plain wooden table with a single file open before each. I crossed my fingers under the table hoping the letter of recommendation from Madame BX had arrived in time. The headmistress primed me to expect questions relating to the challenges of being head girl.

No introductions: 'Do you have anyone from your family who trained at Bart's?'

'Oh, yes,' I beamed: 'My sister is a student nurse here.'

No beams back: 'So, you do not have anyone medical here and you have no one in your family that became a doctor?'

'No.'

'No more questions. Thank you. The usher will see you out.'

What a disappointment. The interview lasted less than five minutes after confirming my full name. I assumed my own achievements would carry the day. For the second time (Chapter 1. 'So, you want to be a doctor?'), strangers decided in minutes my future based on family circumstances, not ability and resolve to succeed.

My time at Bart's ended for the day. As my sister was training outside of London, I had no reason to linger and no money for sight-seeing. I asked the gatekeeper for directions to Paddington train station. On arrival in Bath, I took the familiar train back to Bradford-on-Avon and arrived home in time for supper.

As with the 11-Plus, I had no opinion as to whether I would pass or fail. To my surprise given the perfunctory interview, Bart's medical school offered a place - conditional, as expected, on achieving a top A-level grade in physics. I had one foot inside the door, but this body felt outside. Would King's College treat me the same way? I felt deflated but undeterred.

Fortunately, King's College Hospital Medical School (KCHMS) shone through. The interviewers introduced themselves and were firm but friendly. They allowed time to speak. They acknowledged my life-long passion to become a doctor, no doubt mentioned in the school's recommendation letter. They offered a place, there and then, conditional, as with Bart's, on 'acing' physics A-level. The medical student ushers were enthusiastic as they showed us around the hospital and newly built wing. The hospital for clinical studies and access to patients is situated in South London in a working-class area at that time. The hospital serves a large catchment of patients of diverse ethnicities and socioeconomic backgrounds, including working-class – my people.

Also, I warmed to being part of King's College London (KCL), a multi-faculty university and mixing with students reading diverse subjects rather than only medicine. Pre-clinical medical students took courses at KCL on the Strand, a stone's throw from Trafalgar Square, Covent Garden and other hallmarks of this great city. Across from KCL, banners outside the London School of Economics (LSE), a separate institution in 1968, advocated 'Peace' and 'End the Vietnam War'.

Madame BX smiled, a rare event, when I told her that King's College offered me a conditional place 'on the spot'. With her prominent Irish accent, she replied 'Of course, yees, King's Cooollege,' and, for encouragement, repeated this softly on occasion as we passed each other in corridors and before assembly. Madame BX never revealed that King's had been Jocelyn Corrigan's first choice for medical school, a fact I learned from 'Madame Iggy' a decade later.

Now, with one eye on the prize, I kept my head down at home as well as school. Fingers remained crossed I would complete the school year. My daily ringing of the assembly bell signified start of the final lap. I could see the finish line.

Chapter 5: Beware – do not feed; this specimen is rare

Pupils attending the convent grammar high school in the gentrified city of Bath considered us odd. My sister and I looked different. We towered in height over teachers and pupils. Our dark tans from years abroad contrasted with the lily-white skins favoured by the British elite. The UK considered our pierced ears unfashionable, especially in children. People called us gypsies as they stared at our ears – pierced by an ayah (Malay maid) in Singapore before my sixth birthday. We had dark, thick hair worn in multiple plaits (braids), Ukrainian style, on top of the head. Unleashed, these pigtails fell to waist level. Short hair was in fashion.

We spoke differently from our peers. Our accents and expressions, with a fruit-salad blend of intonations and vocabularies, reflected the diverse countries lived from the army days, the mix of military and local schools attended and being raised by a Canadian-Ukrainian mother. We used hand gestures to communicate - a necessity when living a decade among people without a shared language.

Classmates spent holidays broadening their minds, taking in culture, the arts and learning to horse ride and ski. We spent holidays in our back garden and rode bicycles around the neighbourhood. Recommended reading lists meant buying books. At home, we had no books, no refrigerator, and no telephone. School breaks between lessons would hum with talk about classmates' latest upscale holiday adventures. Our tales outlined the disruptions we encountered in Singapore, India, Beirut, Bahrain and Cyprus. Few listened. Near-death experiences were no match against carefree adventures in Paris, skiing in the Alps, touring the Vatican or visiting Lourdes.

Father, a career enlisted soldier in the Royal Army Ordnance Corps (RAOC), provided supplies, including ammunition, to military branches. Not surprisingly, we found ourselves in troubled areas of the world. After three-plus years of bombings, food rations, curfew restrictions, disrupted schooling and attending endless funerals and memorial parades in Cyprus, our senses were heightened to any unusual noises, smells and disturbances.

My sister, Mary, two classes ahead, took science lessons. One day, a small explosion occurred in the chemistry laboratory. Her classmates carried on unperturbed with their experiments. The military taught us from an early age to duck, take cover or flee under threat. Mary displayed this well-honed flight reaction. She bolted out of the classroom and hid under the furniture, causing much amusement. The teacher, aware of our history, tried to explain her circumstances but the pupils only laughed: 'silly girl.' Mary's reaction cemented the wide-held belief that we were not just odd. We were very odd.

Her classmates decided to play a prank. Mary's reading glasses disappeared mysteriously. By coincidence, our two classes gathered in the basilica cloakroom during break time. I overheard some classmates laughing over Mary's double distress – losing costly glasses and struggling to read:

'What fun to see Mary squinting to read!'

They continued to laugh and joke as I approached the crowd. Despite my towering height, I posed no threat to them, the shy, timid sister – a 'blue-stocking' known for burying her nose in schoolbooks. Silently, I stepped up, grabbed the main culprit by the shirt collar and tie, lifted her up to my eye level and slammed her against the wall:

'You will give back my sister's glasses immediately, do you hear?' She fainted in fright. Her classmates scattered. The glasses appeared above Mary's locker in time for the next class. No-one at school troubled us again.

My sister, wiser by years and with an engaging personality, became the great 'all-rounder' at school - good at lessons, sociable and well-liked by pupils and staff. In addition, she excelled at sports, a talent our peers rated highly. Mary became popular and made lifelong friends. By contrast, I continued to keep to myself, head down with both eyes focused on the prize – resolute to excel in the requisite subjects for university medical school entrance.

As the years passed, I climbed academically from near the bottom of the bottom entry class to within the top tier. The school placed major emphasis on the arts especially history and languages. Of more than one hundred girls in the senior years (sixth forms: years 12 to 14), only a handful took physics, mathematics or chemistry at university entrance level. In the 1960's, medical school, especially for a female, required top grades at A-level in three main science subjects: biology, chemistry and, especially, physics (e.g., three 'A's' or two 'A's' and a 'B' – with fingers crossed). Given these requirements, science subjects replaced any lessons aimed at broadening an education. Music, drama, and sports went by the wayside by age 15 years. We could not afford extracurricular privately funded activities such as elocution and dance. The nuns advised I rationalise the need to relinquish Arts and extracurricular activities to concentrate on the sciences. When I approached what should have been the final two years of high school (school years 12 and 13), my grades in the sciences were sufficiently, and consistently, good. The nuns expected me to 'do very well - even well enough.'

Mother struggled to pay the school fees. The cost of living rose without any compensatory increase in army family allowance. This weekly stipend ran out before the week's end. She took part-time work as a nurses' aide and cleaner at local hospitals to pay for school-related needs, especially the fees. Unbeknown to her, I counted the cash set aside and kept in a jug in the kitchen cupboard. I noted silently and often a shortfall. She paid a 'social' visit to the nuns as a new school term loomed. Mother made the excuse to bring us fruit when, all along, she came to school to ask the nuns for leniency and time to make up the financial deficit.

As I planned applications for medical school, the nuns announced that pupils taking physics at A-level required one extra year, through year 14, to complete the syllabus. In my time, physics A level was mandatory by many university admissions programs for medical school and remains one of the school subjects least chosen by female pupils. The school offered a limited physics program with a part-time teacher. Only three out of more than 150 girls in the sixth form aimed to take physics at A-level. Finding any physics teacher was a challenge let alone a female who could teach at advanced level. No male teachers passed within the convent school walls.

This two-step approach to staggering the A-level examinations over consecutive years would enhance my chances of top grades but at great cost to our home situation. An additional year for physics meant more fees and home expenses. Father faced retirement. We faced misery, violence, and fear of his threats to pull me out of school as he came home more often. The chances of our parents staying together dwindled by the day. Mary left home to start nursing school in London, taking with her that sunny disposition. In the late 1960's nursing school was highly competitive, required two to three good grades at A-level and waiting a year on a short list for a coveted training place. Her lucky number came up. She departed to a new and happier life, released from our 'prison without bars' - a phase often used at home.

Throughout the six years at high school (years 9-14), father visited only twice and both times without my immediate knowledge. The first occurred after my 17th birthday during early preparations for the first batch of A-levels - biology and chemistry. He arrived unannounced at the convent demanding I leave school for good. This visit coincided with his turning physically violent towards me and more so to mother. In his view, I had long overstayed the need for education. He left school by 13 years of age with 'enough education to do well,' as he believed. I learned from the nuns of his visit the following year, with A grades in A-level chemistry and biology under my belt. They downplayed the event. Mother superior and the headmistress met with him 'briefly'. He departed 'abruptly'. Nothing was mentioned at home. (Second visit; Chapter 6. 'Two weeks to go').

We could not risk my sitting the physics A-level examination when only two-thirds through the syllabus. A few pupils retook A-levels to improve their grades, but 're-sits' mostly were undertaken after leaving school. As with the 11-plus exam (Chapter 1. 'So, you want to be a doctor?'), I had one chance, no repeat sitting. Why this sink-or-swim option?

Outside financial support, such as a bank loan, may have been possible in the late 1960s especially for someone pursuing a prestigious and financially secure career such as medicine. Not so for my family. We had no savings, no bank account and, therefore, no recognition with any lender. A bank or mortgage society required proof of regular savings before granting any loan. The family post office savings account stood at zero and served only to cash redeemable vouchers from the army - the weekly family allowance automatically deducted from father's wages. Credit cards were a future invention. Moreover, our family was of the generation that paid everything in cash up front, nothing on credit (called the 'never, never' in those days). We considered shameful owing money. Mother felt this shame acutely during the frequent visits to the convent to plead patience over the school fees. A financial loan, even if possible, would have been anathema.

Father envisioned my future as a farmhand working in Ireland. We never discussed medical school or other higher education options with him. He gave no response to my initial A level results: 'Passed with flying colours – two straight A's. Only one more to go for medical school.'

The final, 14th, year at high school began the week I turned 18 years of age. Time passed slowly as our home-life deteriorated but quickly as I faced the hurdle of physics at A-level. The nuns recommended I take a fourth subject, zoology, at A-level and Scholarship (S) level to dilute the narrow focus of physics day-in, day-out.

Although now the head girl, in many ways, school continued as before with the prime focus on passing physics. Covering the complete examination syllabus remained a challenge despite the extra year. The physics teacher, Mrs Lywood, remained part-time. More than once, lessons were postponed when she became unavailable.

Our school followed the Oxford Board of A-level examinations, one of several governing bodies in the UK. Repeatedly, I approached Mrs Lywood: 'I need more practice at exam questions. Are there any other test questions from another Board of Examiners?' We had exhausted the test sets available from the Oxford Board.

Mrs Lywood encouraged me: 'You will do well, no need to worry.' But I did. Practice makes perfect. Reluctantly at first, she agreed to mark my responses to test questions available from another Board. Later, she remarked that, in all her decades of teaching, no pupil asked for more, rather than less, homework, especially physics.

The physics A-level was one of the last subjects to be examined at the end of the 1969 school year. Most pupils taking the arts finished their exams early. They waited impatiently for the end of the summer term with one foot out of the door in anticipation of summer holidays and celebrations for completing high school. The school saw no need to celebrate graduation at the end of any school year – families planned enough events.

My ultimate hurdle loomed. Days passed in the school library alone poring over the extra homework. Prefects congregated in their small communal room opposite the library, ostensibly to discuss organisational issues within the school. I would peer around the door to convey messages from the staff but never ventured inside. I, the head prefect, remained the outsider.

Prefects and pupils alike knew not to bother me when in the library. I sat alone near the entrance to respond to any issue as head girl but with my back to the door to concentrate on physics. One day, I heard giggling and laughter outside the library door. I turned around but only saw smiling faces peering in through the glass window. Unperturbed, I returned to the books. Again, more giggling. The pupils scattered before I opened the door.

Bold print on a large sheet of paper pinned to the outside of the library door read: 'Beware - do not feed; this specimen is rare

Chapter 6: Two weeks to go

In the early summer of 1969, the daily routine of going to school to prepare for exams despite no further lessons, provided an antidote to the deteriorating situation at home. Father, due to retire within weeks from the Army after 25 years of service, coveted his unblemished record in uniform above all. Our outward appearance of harmony concealed and enabled the escalating domestic violence.

Amid this dysfunction, the A-level science examinations began in May 1969. By early June, I had completed all written physics papers. Only two examinations remained: the A-level physics practical, accounting for a third of overall marks (score), and zoology at Scholarship (S) level, denoting an advanced level beyond regular A-level. Lacking in confidence and with low self-esteem, I dared not assess my chances of obtaining a top grade in physics. The written papers 'went well so far, under the circumstances.' I approached the pending physics practical with mixed feelings; dread, given the limited equipment and practice sessions, and excitement at soon clearing the last hurdle before casting the die on my career chances and a better life.

Tensions rose further when father retired and came home. He said little. We lived separate lives with me counting down the hours as well as the days to freedom. Over the years mother talked about divorce but failed to follow through for several reasons. While father remained in active military service, she feared for our lives especially if she tarnished his career with a divorce. As a devout convert, condemnation of divorce by the Catholic church weighed heavily on mother. In the 1960s, by law for a divorce one had to prove a cause such as adultery, cruelty or abandonment among other factors. We had no physical evidence to support a claim. We never lodged a complaint at a police station. No hospital or doctor documented the bruises and black eyes. There were no witnesses. We suspected adultery but had no proof. We spent years covering our tracks and concealing any tell-tale signs of disharmony.

Moreover, regardless of proof and a 'successful' divorce, the law favoured the husband. In our circumstances, the wife would lose the home and financial support. Our mother dreamed of returning to Canada after I left home despite being estranged from her relatives and having no independent means. Her plans beyond my aspirations were limited. Pride mixed with shame prevented her from asking for help. We lived day-to-day and, in June 1969, hour by hour.

With 336 hours remaining before finishing high school. I comforted myself silently: 'At least dad is unlikely to pull me out of school, so near to the end.' The final physics exam, a three-hour practical set of laboratory experiments, loomed in three days-time. Towards the end of the school day, the headmistress sought me out. By then, I read her moods and expressions without fear of admonishment. Her face showed concern and compassion: 'You cannot go home. Your mother is safe. A neighbour in your town telephoned the convent. Your mother is with the Sisters of Charity up the road. Here is the address and money for your bus fare. Go now and quickly. You are dismissed for the day.' I needed no further explanation. Our family, conditioned over the years, never sought help. At least mother was alive.

I opted to run rather than wait for a bus. As I hurried the mile up a steep hill to the convent of the Sisters of Charity, I knew something dreadful must have happened for mother to engage a neighbour in our family troubles. In earlier times of severe domestic abuse, she ran towards various neighbours' houses but always stopped short before their gates, of calling the police or filing an official report. What was different this time? I later learned from the nuns that the neighbour telephoned the police after mother fled the house following father's latest round of violence and threats with a kitchen knife. Until that day in 1969, only the school nuns knew of our domestic circumstances. Involving the police meant no going back.

Mother and I spoke little of the day's events. Back to soldiering on and in silence. No working through problems. The Sisters of Charity provided rooms in the adjoining nurses' home. They fed us in the communal dining room. As before, we lived day-to-day, focused on the final hurdles of my completing the exams. I wore my only clothes, the one summer school uniform, until the nuns found clothes to fit. Mother dutifully washed by hand and pressed the dress before dawn, this time in the main laundry. The nuns put her to work as a nurses' aide and later, a cleaner in the nurses' home. This strategy distracted her from our tenuous situation and earned our keep. I learned months later from the Sisters of Charity that the police visited the school to warn the nuns of threats by father who assumed we stayed at the La Sainte Union Convent. Father made clear to the school nuns via the police that we were denied access to 'his' home in Bradford-on-Avon and all personal belongings.

While sheltering with the Sisters of Charity and under police surveillance, unbeknown to us at the time, father paid his second visit to the high school. On the first visit, eighteen months before, he attempted to pull me out of school – 'a waste of time and money.' (Chapter 5. 'Beware - do not feed; this specimen is rare'). His excuse this second time was to deliver a hockey stick he said I left behind. The school nuns saw through the irony with one week left in the final school year syllabus. I left hockey behind four years before. They knew he denied our access to collect even essential items from 'his' house. We lived in the clothes on our backs; my summer uniform and, for mother, the simple skirt and blouse worn when she ran from the house for the last time. The nuns mentioned his 'very brief' visit in passing only after I completed all examinations. They dismissed him promptly at the front door with hockey stick in hand. The school nuns concealed our whereabouts. They notified the local police to file a trespassing order.

Meanwhile, and unaware of his recent visit, on the following day, I walked into the final A-level exam, the physics practical. Separate laboratory benches displayed individual experiments; a choice of 'Light' or 'Heat'. The instruction booklet for these experiments seemed unintelligible to me. My two gifted classmates, later to read physics and chemistry respectively, at university, settled down promptly with the apparatus. I stared blankly at the booklet.

After several minutes I turned to the final page and saw two experiments in electromagnetism. My eyes turned to one, the Wheatstone Bridge, which, in 1969, meant a simple Metre Bridge to measure the resistance of an unknown resistor.

Yes, I know this. With a silent sigh of relief, I announced: 'I will do the Wheatstone Bridge. But where is the equipment?' The exam adjudicator and Mrs Lywood, the physics teacher, looked surprised, knowing our class covered this topic once and only in theory. We focused on heat and light for much of the final year.

'Are you sure you want to do that?' Mrs Lywood, a gentle, softly spoken woman, asked in a whisper as forcefully as possible given the silence mandatory in the exam room. The adjudicator stopped the clock. Both stared at me, eyebrows raised.

Given a nod for 'yes' from me, and another concerted glare from them, Mrs Lywood rushed over to a locked cupboard and retrieved an old Wheatstone Bridge. Her facial expression conveyed alarm as her eyes met mine. She handed over the equipment via the adjudicator after removing some dust and cleared a laboratory bench. The exam clock restarted.

After all these years, I understand better why I made the unlikely, and high-risk, choice of the untested Wheatstone experiment despite hours of practice on heat and light. I followed logically the steps outlined in the written instructions. The measurements and calculations worked; 256 divided by 8 equals 32, a whole number. I remember the numbers 50 years later.

To Mrs Lywood's further dismay I handed in the paper earlier than scheduled as my two colleagues pored over their experiments. Eyebrows raised again, she whispered with emphasis, 'There are thirty minutes more.'

'No. I am done.' Outwardly, I felt confident I completed the exam. Inwardly, I wondered if the calculations, far too easy, warranted an 'A' grade. Exam protocol dictated I leave for the day after handing in the paper. No opportunity arose to say goodbye and thanks to classmates and physics teacher.

As I climbed the hill to the Sisters of Charity, I prayed thanks to Mrs Lywood for the many test responses she reviewed and corrected during those extra homework assignments, including the Wheatstone bridge, and going beyond Ohm's Law ($V=RI$).

The Zoology S level examination brought relief after physics. I knew I did well – 'well enough.' However, the only result that guaranteed my university place was a top grade in physics. I already 'aced' biology and chemistry the year before.

Home life, now convent life, with the Sisters of Charity, remained stressful as mother struggled to come to terms with her perilous situation. These nuns provided a roof over our heads, meals and second-hand clothes but no money. Father refused to communicate directly. He sent threatening letters via his solicitor (lawyer) denying access to home. While I looked forward to the exam results and escape from our situation, mother saw no light at the end of her tunnel. She faced an uphill battle to claim any rights to money or property.

As head girl, the school nuns mandated my daily attendance until the end of the term, regardless of finishing with exams. I welcomed attending school as a distraction. School remained my safe harbour over the years. A week later, without ceremony, I handed in the head girl's sash (girdle) to a nun tasked with collecting school property.

'Keep the head girl badge, as a reminder,' - as if I would forget.

I walked for the last time through the convent grounds. En route, I crossed the old tennis courts, passed by several statues of saints and quietly closed the gate. The summer school term in 1969 ended and with it my schooldays. Few pupils and staff remained by then. There were no goodbyes. No celebrations.

The school merged eventually with Cardinal Newman, a Comprehensive school nearby, after more than a century as La Sainte Union Convent, a girls-only grammar high school. The newly merged co-educational school, St. Gregory's Comprehensive, later a college, came to life a decade later and moved to another location near Bath. These delays were unforeseen in 1969. In my final year, the atmosphere was one of winding down. The school stopped taking in new pupils. Several lay teachers and nuns, including the headmistress, planned their exit along with mine. Some left early. A future 'Co-Ed' Comprehensive, not grammar, school broke their last straw.

Twenty years later (1989), the main convent building on North Parade Road became a magistrate's court. The building is noteworthy as an example of unusual Victorian Gothic (John Elkington Gill, architect 1866-7) and singled out as a local landmark during double-decker city bus tours (Chapter 17. 'Didn't we do well?!').

Chapter 7: With gratitude to teachers and strangers

More than half-a century ago in August 1969, I faced a major hurdle – the physics A-level examinations and result. Any grade less than the top, an 'A' grade, would relegate me to an unknown future due to our personal circumstances. I had no contingency plans – no plan 'B', should I fail to gain a place in medical school.

Mother and I had 'fallen on hard times', a euphemistic phase for the summer of 1969. Father forced us out of our home amid these final A-level examinations. Our parents endured an unhappy marriage for as long as my sister and I could remember and before according to mother. The antagonisms and violence came to a head with two weeks to go at high school and three days before the all-important physics A-level practical. Mother ran out of the house for the final time to escape his abuse. Consequently, we became homeless and penniless although, fortunately, not 'out on the street'. The convent high school nuns and Sisters of Charity, a nearby order at St. Catherine's convent, came to our rescue with food, clothes and shelter.

The legal battles started soon after our arrival at St. Catherine's convent (Chapter 6. 'Two weeks to go'). Mother filed through a solicitor to claim personal items from the house, including my trunk holding new clothes and essentials for university. Over several years, she diligently and methodically accumulated this 'dowry' in anticipation of medical school. After two months with the Sisters of Charity and several exchanges between solicitors via the school, father granted permission for me to retrieve my precious trunk. He stipulated with emphasis I come alone to the back door of '*his house*' on '*his*' specified day. He barred me from entering '*his house*' and emphasised he would not open the front door, no doubt considered '*his*' door.

Mr Stone, the local greengrocer in Bradford-on-Avon, volunteered to transport the trunk back to Bath. I knew him only as the man with a van.

On the appointed day, and with the local police patrol car in view, I knocked repeatedly on the back door as instructed. No answer. About to leave empty handed, I noticed the side door to the garage ajar – and, inside, my trunk but no other requested items.

I rummaged inside quickly to confirm the contents. 'Retrieve the trunk, my trunk,' I chanted silently, to quell annoyance at the pettiness - denying my additional requests for an old thermos flask and hot water bottle.

Mr Stone and I carried and loaded the trunk into the van parked in front of the house. As a quiet, thoughtful person he said little. Nods and smiles showed he understood the situation.

The front door opened. My father watched us. He called out within earshot of Mr Stone, the police and neighbours: 'You can always come back if you need anything else.' Determined to show resolve and control my surging anger and frustration, I glared in his direction and replied as coldly and loudly as I could muster: 'There is nothing to come back for.' For emphasis, I turned my back on him, no longer afraid. Let the onlookers note my reaction and disgust. These were the final words we exchanged.

By denying hopes and aspirations, my father abandoned me long ago. More accurately, I felt a life-long void since abandonment indicates some prior connection. In turn, I intended my cold response to signal I slammed shut the door on any future interaction. Thirty-eight years passed before we met and spoke again, prompted by a happy occasion when he walked a beloved niece down the aisle.

Once out of sight of the house, the tears and sobs of relief flowed freely as I waved 'all clear' to the police car. The torrent of emotions released a lifetime of tensions. *Now I am free of him. No more fear.* Mr Stone did not query what happened or my need for his assistance that day. However, more silent nods and smiles spoke volumes as I ploughed through his box of tissues. This person showed more kindness and compassion in one afternoon than my father had in 18 years. He refused money towards the petrol: 'Just happy to help out.'

I learned later that mother regularly owed money to Mr Stone's shop. She would exhaust funds before the end of the week and pay him retrospectively with the next military allowance. Mother depended on this credit system for years. In turn, Mr Stone trusted her to pay in full. He never mentioned this the day I needed his help.

While awaiting the exam results, I found temporary work as a shop assistant in Woolworth's - too late in the season to apply for a well-paid summer job or one to enhance my resumé. The Sisters of Charity provided food and shelter but no income. Our weekly military allowance stopped when father retired from the army in June. We had no access to his military pension. With my weekly wages of seven pounds, I bought essential items and saved towards two train-fares to London for university that autumn - fingers crossed.

In 1969, assistants in Woolworth's served from behind a counter - no self-service check-outs. Standing all day to serve demanding customers awakened me to the real world of aching feet, physical exhaustion and the daily struggle of low-paid workers, including mother, to make ends meet. I covered the haberdashery counter. The workday passed cutting lengths of elastic, lace and ribbons on demand and counting out safety pins and buttons for customers. Mood in the shop fluctuated according to the weather. Grumpy customers came in from the rain. Cheerful ones meant sunshine outside. Nuns from school came into Woolworth's occasionally to buy small items and encourage me to look forward. None of my former classmates came into the shop.

Exam results were released to pupils on a Thursday in mid-August. Accordingly, I paid no extra attention when Madame BX, the headmistress, and mother superior came to Haberdashery two days earlier. They bought some minor items. After handing back some change, mother superior gave a signal to Madame BX to speak:

'You have the A-level grades for medical school – a straight A and S with distinction in zoology, and, of course, an A in physics – well deserved.' With a simple smile and nod of acknowledgement but without further ado, they turned around and quietly left.

For a moment I stood in disbelief, cards of elastic and pins in hand. As if this were yesterday, I recall vividly my reaction more than half a century later. Joy, which transcends happiness, overcame me followed by relief. The whole shop heard my reaction: 'I have made it. I am going to medical school...to King's College ....to London. I am going to be a doctor. I have made it. I have made it!'

The ruckus alarmed the manager who rushed onto the shop floor. Assistants and customers crowded around Haberdashery, showering congratulations, patting me on the back: 'Well done.'

I wanted the world to hear: 'I must tell my mother. I am going to medical school. To London. To King's. I have made it!'

With no way of contacting mother directly, the manager released me from work that day with full pay. He congratulated me as we walked to the door to a chorus of 'Well done.' Employees and customers cheered me out of the shop and into the street. My heart soared at strangers wished me well. The thrill of telling mother 'I have made it!' spurred me on.

As I hurried to my temporary home a mile away and up a steep hill, I began to see the selfishness of my reaction. For many shop assistants, their job working behind the counter was their future. I was passing through, counting down the days and, more recently, the hours. The assistants, selfless in their enthusiasm, encouraged and supported me. That day, more opportunities opened for me than many would see in their lifetimes. Moreover, the many people who supported us along the way, especially the school and Sisters of Charity, deserved credit for helping us clear the final lap. The sacrifices our mother made over the years to support her daughters' dreams came sharply into focus. She put any aspirations aside to support us. I did not make it alone – We made it together.

I reached the convent in record time and breathless from exertion. I rushed around the nurses' home to find mother with a bucket and mop cleaning the floor:

'Mum, we made it. I got the A in physics. I am going to King's. We made it!'

Let this be her well-deserved victory lap: 'Go tell the nuns – We made it.' Mother downed the mop and headed for the convent. The nuns congratulated her. They knew how much overcoming this hurdle meant.

With another month to work at Woolworth's, the shop assistants took up my cause, counting down the days: 'Oh, Elizabeth, only 24 days to go. No, 23 days.' They enquired about university, medical school, King's College London and the sacrifices to become a doctor. They marvelled at my looking forward to 'all those years of studying.' For me looking back, all those years studying in a world-class college within the heart of one of the greatest cities in the world remains among the most exciting chapters in my life.

On my final day at Woolworths at the end of August 1969, the shop assistants and manager cheered me out of the door once more: 'Well done......Good luck... Congratulations.' I left for university with a newly found appreciation for my good fortune from the encouragement and selflessness of teachers and strangers. Fifty years later, this gratitude to pay it forward remains with me.

Chapter 8: King's College London (1969-1972); medical school, firsts

In September 1969, my 19th birthday passed without celebration, living among the Sisters of Charity. As a family, we rarely celebrated birthdays or anniversaries. A Christmas present meant larger size shoes or socks to keep pace with our ever-growing needs. Growing up, I had no experience handling money except for small coins to jingle briefly on an errand to the local shop for extra milk or bread and to pay for lunch money at school. My sister and I never received pocket money or a windfall to spend as we pleased. We did not feel deprived. Our uncluttered lives required little in extras. This year I celebrated silently at no longer being a financial burden to mother. No more school fees. With days to spare, Avon, our newly adopted county, agreed to pay for my higher education instead of Wiltshire, the County for Bradford-on-Avon where we had lived until recently. A welcome birthday present and sigh of relief.

All eyes focused on my pending departure for London. Unlike many teenagers, I relished spending at least four more years as a student despite the challenges of high school. London awaited with all the opportunities this global city offered. Moreover, I would be near my 'big' sister, Mary, in nurses' training school at St. Bartholomew's hospital. Our tight bond forged from living in foreign lands strengthened as conflicts raged outside and within our family. Mary sheltered me from those storms. I remain her 'little' sister.

Thus, on a sunny autumn day in September 1969, mother and I stepped off the train onto the platform at Paddington station in London. Mary greeted us and navigated the way across London to my new home, Canterbury Hall, an intercollegiate university residence near King's Cross. I felt on top of the world and wealthy, armed with 50 pounds, representing seven weeks of wages from Woolworth's. The nuns generously paid for our train fares, a saving of two weeks' wages. Furthermore, the County of Avon awarded 600 pounds per annum to cover my expenses - the full student grant for low-income families. This sum exceeded our annual family military allowance for three people when we lived at home. The County separately paid for board and lodging in Hall. I had arrived.

Swept up in the excitement and buzz as other students arrived at the Hall, I happily waved goodbye to Mary and mother. The next few days and Freshers' week are a blur. Settling in, I met students reading diverse subjects across London University. I walked down Kingsway to King's College London (KCL) on the Strand taking in the sights and smells of London. In 1969, medical students from Westminster, and St. George's, Medical Schools joined KCL for pre-clinical training. On day one of classes, Professor Arnstein, Head of Biochemistry, announced the date of the Second MB (*Medicinae Baccalaureus*, Batchelor of Medicine) examinations eighteen months hence, a requirement to progress to three years of clinical training at our respective hospitals. A-levels counted as First MB. Medical finals (third and fourth MB, with added Batchelor of Surgery [BS]) denoted qualification (graduation) as a doctor after three years clinical training.

Some students complained that pre-clinical medical school resembled high school with a full roster of classes and multiple tests and exams. In contrast, students reading non-medical subjects typically enjoyed free time interspersed with two or three formal lectures and tutorials per week. I viewed our full program as par for the course. To me medicine is a vocation entailing a life-long apprenticeship and decades of learning to practice and hone this craft.

Entrance into medical school remains highly competitive across the world. In the UK, by the late 1960s, the front door for women began to open more than in prior decades but only for those with outstanding accomplishments at A-levels and beyond. In my first year, female students represented a quarter of the intake from the three medical schools. The 'boys' respected us 'girls' knowing the extra high hurdles we cleared to share their space. Not surprisingly, we girls typically occupied the front rows of the lecture theatres, took copious notes, rarely skipped classes and regularly came top, or near, of the class. I was in my element.

High school in no way prepares one for medical school. In 1969, the pre-clinical program threw freshmen into the deep end. I came up swimming, wanting more and quickly found my sea legs. In the first week, we faced anatomical dissection on human cadavers. A male student promptly fainted within minutes upon entering through the swing doors.

Anatomical dissection filled many days as we worked our way around the wonders of the human body. A group of seven students, including one female, dissected one body. The smell of formaldehyde permeated the upper floors and corridors adjoining the dissection room of KCL. Meanwhile, newly laid tarmac along the Strand added fumes to this pungent aroma. Over the decades, the smell of tar rekindles memories of my time in the dissection room.

Pre-clinical subjects such as anatomy, physiology, biochemistry and pharmacology filled our days. In the 1960s and early 1970s, medical students at most UK medical schools, including in London, never laid hands on a live person during those first eighteen months. The professors, true academics, taught courses far removed from the day-to-day aspects of clinical practice. We yearned for knowledge to apply directly to patients. The months sped by interspersed with many tests and exams. Most pre-clinical students counted down the days to seeing patients, learning clinical practice and earning real money. Not me. I loved being a student. I was rich already. After the effort invested in my precarious journey to medical school and despite an unwavering vocation, I wished to savour every moment. I saw no rush to qualify as a doctor. In many ways, I remain a perpetual student.

My evolution needs to be taken into context. There are several 'firsts'. For the first time, I felt in control of my destiny. For the first time, I had pocket money - and extra to spare. My student grant, based inversely proportional to household income, exceeded those of many others. Some friends of wealthy parents compromised on essentials given their reluctance to ask family for extra funds. I had my own room, another first, and shared a bathroom with only one student. Canterbury Hall supported students to study by providing meals, laundry facilities and cleaners. I needed no encouragement to study. No threats loomed to pull me out of school.

London on my doorstep waited to be explored. A few minutes' walk from Canterbury Hall led into the heart of London. The British Museum, the Courtauld gallery, home to many Impressionist paintings, and Oxford Street were a stone's throw away. KCL is situated on the banks of the Thames River near Waterloo bridge and within walking distance of Covent Garden, the Royal Festival Hall and Trafalgar square. The BBC World Service operated out of Bush House, now part of KCL. Across the road from KCL, the Aldwych Theatre, then a Royal Shakespeare Theatre, donated tickets for students to attend some rehearsals with Dame Judy Dench, Sir John Gielgud and other legendary actors.

The years 1969-1972 were exciting for many reasons. Students from King's and the London School of Economics (LSE), then a separate institution, marched down the Strand to protest the Vietnam war. London, especially Carnaby Street, swept up the world in fashion. Vidal Sassoon revolutionised hairstyles. I watched the building of the Southbank Arts and Theatre complex across the Thames from the Physiology department at the top of the College building, now named the King's building. I began to make friends in Hall. Jenny, a medical student at the Royal Free Hospital School of Medicine, remains one of my closest to this day.

Once the excitement of being a first-year medical student passed, I came down to earth. Our mother's situation began to weigh on me. Jenny would meet the train at Paddington station on my return from a visit to Bath, knowing I would be depressed. She supported me emotionally as I wrestled with guilt over mother's situation. My stars - opportunities and good fortune – rose steadily. Mother's galaxy grew dimmer with the passing months. The Sisters of Charity generously provided a room when Mary or I took turns to visit. Mother's room in the nurses' home measured less than 7 square metres. The nuns provided food, lodging and a small stipend in return for working as a cleaner. That stipend paid for cigarettes. Not much to show for a 50-plus-year-old and two decades of a miserable and abusive marriage.

Mother's lot seemed hopeless and made worse by the bad timing of her divorce. In the winter of 1969, she petitioned for divorce on the grounds of cruelty since filing required proof of fault such as cruelty, adultery and abandonment. The Divorce Reform Act of 1969, allowing divorce for a marriage irretrievably broken down (without assigning specific fault), had not filtered through to the Court in Bath. By now, we had independent proof of father's adultery; however, filing for this fault would yield a smaller award by the court. Father did not contest the divorce and defaulted on the hearing. No need to attend. Mother 'won' the case on cruelty as a pyrrhic victory. In 1969 -1970, the court awarded the wife assets only after assessment of essential need. Regardless of her perilous financial state with no personal assets and no home, the court awarded a total of three pounds per week as alimony. The court deemed sufficient this meagre sum based on her having no dependents. Three pounds represented less than one-third of her prior weekly allowance via the army. Moreover, the court denied any provision for shelter, then or in the future, given the roof over her head provided by the nuns.

Mother's burdens continued to mount. As a devout convert to the Catholic faith, she felt ashamed of the failure of the marriage regardless of domestic abuse, her husband's adultery and being exonerated by the court. She carried this shame to her grave. Her perfunctory attempts to contact siblings in Canada for support to return to her homeland failed. Too much water had passed under the bridges of life for any permanent solutions.

The intermittent headaches I suffered since a teenager became more frequent and severe. Again, I lived a double life – as the medical student realising my dreams and the guilty offspring of a parent who sacrificed so much for her daughters' aspirations. The student allowance provided by the government covered living in London but would not stretch to supporting her. Regardless, mother adamantly refused any money, however small the offering.

I felt rich but yearned for a financial safety net – money saved for a rainy day – to buffer the unexpected, given our recent history. This goal for financial security and independence remains with me. Canterbury Hall permitted me to stay on in-between the winter and spring academic terms when the Residence opened to paying visitors. At the end of the 1970 academic year and facing the long summer holiday, I took temporary work as a phlebotomist and laboratory technician at King's College Hospital and moved nearby into a one-room 'bed-sit' in South London. Working in the Haematology Department laboratory filled the void to interact with patients. The laboratory staff, including the head professor, treated me with respect as did the patients. I chuckled when a patient addressed me as 'nurse' or 'doctor' and reluctantly corrected any misgivings: 'Thank you. I am simply Miss - for now.' The mix of scientific (laboratory) and clinical work appealed to me. I envisaged becoming a haematologist. My path would take more twists and turns before that decision. In the end my speciality chose me (Chapter 10. 'From blood to guts').

As second MB exams approached in the summer term of 1971, KCL offered the opportunity to study afterwards for an extra degree, an intercalated Batchelor of Science (BSc), in Physiology, Pharmacology or Biochemistry rather than proceed to clinical training at King's College Hospital. The limited places depended on achieving high grades in the looming examinations. In the 1970's, the Medical Research Council (MRC) offered a few scholarships to cover the additional eighteen months of expenses. I set my sights on pursuing a BSc in Physiology, a popular choice among the pre-clinical subjects.

The second MB exams are a brutal marathon. Students have committed suicide around such times. The rationale must be to discourage all but the stalwart from continuing to three years of clinical training, an expensive pursuit fully funded by the British government in my time. Then, the UK government paid all first-time undergraduate university fees.

Studying medicine in my era, absent the internet, required a photographic memory to imbibe large volumes of texts. Without the internet we could not 'Google' topics. Students learned about the structure and workings of the human body the hard way and by rote after ploughing through books, charts and journals in our 'spare' time in the university's libraries. Meanwhile, the temptations of London beckoned outside.

I placed well in the second MB examinations but fell short by less than one point, coming in seventh for one of six Physiology BSc places. The excitement of clinical training and 'putting hands on patients (at last),' did little to quell the disappointment of losing a BSc opportunity by less than an inch. I prefer to lose by a mile.

Meanwhile, the interviews began for the BSc placings. Months before, I agreed to accompany a fellow student to his interview to study Pharmacology. This shy and nervous colleague doubted his chances despite coming top in that subject. The ushers coordinating the interviews separated us onlookers from the candidates – the sheep from the goats. No names were called – we segregated easily according to dress code. My friend wore the customary simple dark suit, white shirt and plain tie. In typical student style of our times, I 'down' dressed; plain knee-length skirt, a jumper (sweater) that had seen better days and raincoat in need of cleaning. A woollen hat covered hair too long to hide and too short to tie back.

As I waited outside the interview rooms for my colleague, I heard a voice: 'Are you Elizabeth Fagan?'

Oh, dear, has my friend fainted?

'Is my friend O.K.?'

'Yes. Yes. He is fine. He said to find you here. An additional place has come up (for the BSc) in Physiology. Are you still interested?'

No need for words. My elated expression said it all. A star student allocated for Physiology 'defected' into the Pharmacology BSc Program, opening one place for the next in line – me.

'There is no need to interview,' the usher quipped while sizing me up and down disapprovingly and no doubt thinking: 'Typical scruffy student. Happy to spare the interviewers.'

Better news still, the MRC awarded and doubled the regular medical student allowance. And more - the County of Avon extended the year-long public transport pass – a goldmine in value as I traveled between colleges and my residence. That day, the lottery called my number.

Some people can define a period in life when their stars aligned. Mine aligned during the eighteen months studying for a BSc in Physiology. I hit my stride. The course modules excited me. The vast resources of the many colleges and medical schools across London University opened their doors. St. Thomas' hospital medical school, a separate institution before merging with King's in the 1990s, held cell membrane, salt, and water transport studies when these topics were in the news. Along with two other students, I surprised myself by signing up for an applied statistics module at Charing Cross Hospital Medical School, located then in Villiers Street near Trafalgar Square. Despite no exposure at high school, I envisaged the relevance of applied statistics to medical research, epidemiology and the analysis of data. These courses shaped my wish to pursue research and become a physician-scientist. The other students rarely attended, allowing me precious one-on-one time with the tutor, Dr Lewis, a physician dedicated to the application of statistics to medicine. Six years later, I would be grateful for his continuing interest in my career (Chapter 11. 'Physician, heal thyself').

The need to seek alternative accommodation outside of Hall became a priority. Freshmen, understandably, had priority for the limited number of rooms in any student university residence. Living in central London is expensive despite the London Allowance. Many students itched to leave behind the restrictions of Hall and find cheaper accommodation. Not me. Hall life became my sanctuary. While looking for outside 'digs', the warden of Halliday Hall in Clapham, South London approached me to become a founder member. That Hall, newly refurbished, reopened as an all-female university residence. To my delight, I moved into a small suite – studio bedroom/lounge and kitchenette. Mrs Murray, the housekeeper, allowed me to study in a spare room in her apartment. My own suite became a place to relax, devoid of books. I learned years later that the opportunity to live at Halliday Hall during my BSc came through the recommendations of the warden at Canterbury Hall and endorsed by King's.

In 1970, I began weekend work as an assistant librarian in the Department of War Studies at King's on the Strand. I could study physiology in between stacking books and be paid - real pocket money. Perusing the Journal of Physiology, I can across an advertisement:

'Summer Internship (1971) to study anti-diuretic hormone (ADH) available in the Department of Physiology at Albert Einstein College of Medicine, Yeshiva University, New York. Jewish males may apply in writing.'

I applied. Why not? What was there to lose? After two years at university, I overcame the reticence ingrained from home, the army and convent high school to approach those in authority. On reflection, my willingness to apply for this post, no doubt a 'long shot', represented a turning point in my life. I could accept failure – rejection - since there was nothing to lose by applying. I saw no impact on my BSc or subsequent educational opportunities since the work covered the long summer holidays and was independent of King's and the University of London.

To avoid any misunderstanding over gender, I submitted a full-length photograph of me wearing a skirt and blouse and hair tied with large, not-to-overlook, ribbons. In the application letter, after extolling the wonders of salt and water transport based on the Physiology BSc module, I mentioned being raised a Catholic.

Without a further thought about New York, a long shot, I researched other, more realistic, options for the long summer holiday. Six weeks later, a letter of acceptance from New York arrived with a cheque for 1,400 US dollars to cover the three-month internship. This sum of around 600 pounds sterling if exchanged in 1972, equated to a year's worth of my first UK government grant. I had never held so much money in my hand at one time. Albert Einstein reserved and paid for accommodation at the International Students' House near Columbia University rather than the all-male campus in the Bronx.

Professor H.D. Lauson, Chairman of the Department of Physiology and Biophysics and an expert in endocrinology, including salt and water handling, became my supervisor. Next door lived Professor A.Z. Gilman, Chairman of the Department of Pharmacology and renowned for his reference book, *The Pharmacological Basis of Therapeutics*. These celebrated professors welcomed me with their down to earth, easy-going approach. They teased my having a 'very British accent.' Sometimes I struggled to understand theirs. The divergence in language and expressions in America surprised me despite being raised by a Canadian mother. I knew the transatlantic preferences for sidewalk versus pavement, diaper versus nappy; however, 'work' sounded like 'woik' and 'dog,' like 'doag'.

For fun, Professor Lauson requested I answer the office telephone:
'Good morning, how may I assist you?'
'What?!'
Maybe the caller could not hear me. These were the days of rotary dialing telephones and crackling background noises on a landline. A little louder: 'Good morning, I am so sorry. Can you hear me? This is Professor Lauson's office, how may I assist you?'
'Lady, ah hear ev'ry single word ya say – but when ya put 'em together, I ain't gotta clue.'

The professors shared sandwiches in a side room since the campus canteen served only males and Jews. The work ethic of six full days at Albert Einstein impressed me. Work began promptly at 8.00AM and rarely finished before 6.30PM. Like me, many staff and students lived outside the Bronx and travelled by public transport (subway and bus) more than one hour each way. In 1971, several parts of New York, including the Bronx were dangerous and crime ridden. Times Square brought more visitors to its red-light district than other entertainment.

Professor Lauson met the bus and insisted I sit in the subway train carriage occupied by an armed guard: 'Read a book. Do not speak. The guard will not understand you.'

The International Student House – the 'I-House' - at 500 Riverside Drive, Manhattan, near 125th Street is in a salubrious part of Manhattan. Fellow students walked to Columbia University and the Julliard School of Music, opened only two years earlier (1969). Students were outstanding performers in music, dance and theatre. Everyone looked forward to their lucky break. Our interactions, while brief due to the long hours worked, opened my eyes to their world. Students envied my assured career path. After all, medical students became doctors, excepting unusual circumstances. In contrast, these artists, already outstanding in performance and creativity, followed a precarious path. Auditions after years of study and practice, if lucky, led to an anonymous and temporary role as an understudy, in a chorus line, or teaching music to disinterested children. The odds of success in the arts' world are low, regardless of talent. Whereas a medical degree and skill almost certainly assure success in terms of a stable, well-financed career. Many talented artists go hungry. Doctors need not.

In September 1971 while in New York, I turned 21. In keeping with my family's disregard for celebrations, I told no one at work about this milestone. Instead, I headed to the physiology laboratory to repeat a prior research experiment that failed, albeit one that could have waited another day. This preference for work cemented my aim in life – to forge a path as an academic, albeit starting on the lowest rungs of the ladder. That day I planted the seed to become a physician-scientist.

Towards the end of the internship, over our usual sandwich lunch, Professor Lauson thanked me for the work I completed and wished success in my medical career. He continued:

'I would like to write to London University about your internship. Maybe that can help with your physiology degree.'

Stunned by his generosity, I spluttered out: 'Oh, my goodness. Thank you but there is no way that could happen. You see, I took this internship in holiday time. This has nothing to do with the University of London or King's College.'

I assumed he would write a simple letter to the University of London, the governing body for conferring BSc degrees at colleges, including KCL in 1972, acknowledging the internship. Professor Lauson was in the throes of editing and updating 'The Endocrine System,' a chapter in the *Handbook of Physiology*, a noted reference work of multiple sections. I held no aspirations that any scrap of my work would be acknowledged in any form.

I returned to King's and Halliday Hall in the Autumn of 1971 to prepare for the final BSc examinations a few months later. Swept up in practical and theoretical courses, I gave little thought to the American professor's gesture. Our infrequent correspondence focused on the experiments undertaken during the internship.

The summer term of 1972 arrived soon enough with multiple written, practical and *viva voce* exams based on the BSc modules. I, along with one other student, took the practical portion of the statistics exam within a computer bank under Charing Cross Railway Station, near Trafalgar Square. In 1972, computers for businesses occupied whole rooms. I recall sitting at a table with one of two designated typewriter-sized calculators amid multiple machines from ceiling to floor, whirling and humming around. In the 1970s, most diligent students aimed for a 2-1 (upper second class) degree. London University rarely awarded a 'first' (class honours degree). My student colleagues in physiology were exceptionally talented and hard-working. No need to post signs on the library door (Chapter 5. 'Beware - do not feed; this specimen is rare'). We did not query further why the examining board selected three of us for an extra *viva voce* to 'audit' the teaching in our Physiology Department.

The day I finished the final exam paper, I boarded a ferry and sailed across the English Channel to France. My journey continued by train to Germany, courtesy of money saved from the American Internship. Furthermore, a student summer scholarship from Searle paid for two months board and lodging to study in Munich in a haematology research department.

In 1972 with no channel tunnel and a year before joining the European Common Market, a UK citizen required clearance at each border control and multiple currencies. Travellers' checks were a popular way to exchange money into the local currencies. My journey began by taking the Dover-to-Calais ferry. I paid in French francs for a train ticket to Munich. Sleeping berths were prohibitively expensive on a student scholarship. Regardless, to sleep was impossible. Every few hours, the train stopped at a country border. Passengers alighted, some in night attire, to show passports and other documents all under the spotlight of police patrols and barking guard dogs. On arrival in Munich, I went straight to the university to find my supervisor, Professor Hüber in Haematology, and collect a document assigning accommodation in a nearby student house. Dead tired, I looked forward to a shower and sleep. Eventually, I found his office – empty, except for multiple packing boxes scattered in the main area and corridors.

Fortunately, an assistant arrived. Armed with only three phrases in German, I pointed to the invitation letter and note for directions to a student house.

In perfect English, she replied: 'Oh, you are the student. Did you receive the professor's letter?'

'Yes, this is the letter of invitation and .....'

'No. Not that letter. The professor sent you a second letter. He is moving to Innsbruck and expects you to join him in Austria next week. Here is the address of the student house there and the University. Auf Weidersehen.'

Fortunately, my three phrases included 'Good-bye.'

My arrival in Munich in July 1972 coincided with preparations there for the summer Olympics. The city buzzed with excitement. Bright blue banners and flags denoted the Games of the XX Olympiad to open in less than six weeks. Germany last hosted the Olympics in 1938, during the Third Reich. The locals were enthusiastic to put forward their city in a new light. None of us anticipated the events soon to unfold – the massacre beginning the second week (5 September 1972) of the games. A group of Palestinian terrorists (*Black Panthers*) attacked members of the Israeli Olympic team. Several Israelis and a German policeman died.

I spent less than two hours in Munich, being sleep-deprived and lacking the energy to explore this wonderful city. Roller-bags and suitcases on wheels were a design of the future. As I lugged my heavy suitcase around, I made a mental note to travel light in the future.

And so, I cashed in a traveller's check into deutschmarks to pay for a train fare to Innsbruck, checked into the student house and fell asleep – for two days. I took a day off to explore the surroundings and famous old town. Time to try out my other two phrases in German as I greeted a shopkeeper selling sandwiches: 'Guten tag.'

'Nein. Gruss got.'

Back to the dictionary.

He refused the German deutschmarks. Back to the travel bureau to exchange these for Austrian schillings.

Professor Hüber set me to work. His team developed laboratory techniques to label and track white blood cells, an advance in the recently developed fields of cellular Immunology and oncology. This laborious work used radioactive techniques and cell sorters to separate subtypes of blood cells. Our department occupied a whole floor - 'the German' floor, above which was 'the Austrian' floor, working on different blood diseases. I rotated between these floors and entered two worlds. The German researchers worked steadily, meticulously through the day, taking at most 30 minutes break for lunch. The Austrians started one hour later and took two hours for lunch which invariably included driving up into the Seegrube, or Nordkette, mountains. We timed experiments to the minute to accommodate 'lunch.' Unlike New York, these supervisors expected me to enjoy myself. I travelled to Salzburg to sample all things Mozart and taste venison and the famous Salzburger nockerl. The waiter brought enough food to feed three people and shrugged when I licked the plates clean: 'Ah, studentin.'

I returned to London in time for the BSc results and the start of clinical training at King's College Hospital in south London in September 1972. The day came for the results of the BSc In Physiology. We six students assembled in a small room in the Physiology department at KCL. As a distraction, we shared stories about our adventures. Our supervisor, a cheerful and friendly professor, forced a blank expression while handing each student a simple note-sized piece of paper. For me and two others - 'Class I. First Class Honours.' Now we understood the reason for the extra oral examination!

The supervisor, now beaming and delighted with the results reflecting favourably on the department, spoke to us individually: 'Elizabeth, congratulations – we noted the extracurricular module in America, as your American professor was most insistent that we do. This has not happened before. However, you gained high enough marks already in the course modules to be awarded a first.'"

Professor Lauson at the Albert Einstein had gone 'the extra mile' and corresponded with several examiners for London University. Moreover, he sent over to Senate House the original laboratory logbooks as proof of my work and requested these be included as a course unit towards the final BSc examinations. Among scientists, the logbook is revered and not to be copied or removed from the laboratory, let alone the institution. Before leaving the Albert Einstein, I insisted on handing in my logbooks directly to the professor. King's retrieved the logbooks from the examining body. I duly returned these by classified mail with enough stamps and insurance labels to adorn the packaging. The professor acknowledged their safe return, enclosing a copy of his chapter in the *Handbook of Physiology*. On the final page he acknowledged my contribution. Another first.

As with my A-level results, I wanted mother to be the first to hear about the degree results. She had little good news in her life. A few months earlier, she plucked up the courage to take an independent step to better her lot. After three years at St. Catherine's Convent working to keep a roof over her head and minimal stipend, she accepted a position as housekeeper to senior nursing administrators at the Royal United Hospitals (RUH) in Bath. The offer came with wages and an upscale room in their house.

Armed with a bag of half-crowns and shillings to feed the public telephone, I dialled the number:

'Good afternoon, I need to speak to Mrs Fagan.'

'Who?'

'Mrs Fagan, the housekeeper. She works in your house, for the senior nursing administrator.'

'Don't know that name. Hold the line, I need to transfer you to the main hospital.'

Puzzled, I held on trying to curb my excitement and believing I had been given the wrong number. After several clicks and crackles, and more coins fed into the telephone box, the operator transferred me back to the main switchboard: 'RUH, how may I help you?'

'I would like to speak with Mrs Fagan....I am....'

'Please hold the line. I am transferring you to that hospital section.'

'Hello, how may I help you?'

'I need to speak to Mrs Fagan....'

'Hold on while I look down the corridor.'

I held on while thinking – what corridor? The background noise made any conversation difficult. Footsteps, trolleys rattling by and various voices in conversation came through the telephone receiver.

My bag of coins ran low.

More voices at the other end. And then I overheard a background conversation:

Voice 1: 'Who's that on the line?'

Voice 2: 'Oh, someone looking for Fagan. No, don't bother to go. Close the 'phone. She's only a cleaner.'

When we eventually connected the following day, I learned that due to shortages of domestics in the RUH, the administration transferred mother to clean the long open hospital corridors. This required different accommodation - a downgrade to a small room in a Nissen-style hut on the hospital grounds.

Although excited about my BSc results, mother's life revolved around the daily grind of laborious work. More than before she became resigned to her lot in life. Mother refused to challenge her employer to improve working conditions and avoided making any plans to better her conditions. She complained that the hospital would not provide accommodation for me when I visited.

An added blow to both of us came when Mary, now a qualified nurse at St. Bart's, and engaged to a New Zealander, emigrated to New Zealand a month later in October 1972. Mother came to London that day to meet Mary's fiancé and simultaneously say goodbye. With practiced smiles, we waved as Mary, radiating happiness, took her sunshine halfway across the globe. We lost from our immediate orbit a third of our family that day.

The urgent search for accommodation near the hospital began on my return from Austria in September 1972. KCL friends from our pre-clinical days already were into their second clinical year at the hospital and settled with their flat mates. I did not know the area or anyone free to share a flat with me. Memories of the army days came back, living out of a suitcase in a spare room, albeit this time supported by Mrs Murray, the housekeeper at Halliday Hall.

To no avail, I combed local newspapers and windows of newsagent shops near the hospital for suitable, affordable accommodation. With less than a week to go before starting clinical training, while passing through the clinical medical school adjacent to the hospital on Bessemer Road, a postcard on the noticeboard advertised: *'Room for rent with elderly lady in walking distance of King's College Hospital. Please telephone Mrs Buxton but not before October 1972.'*

Oh dear, a month too early. Once more, I asked myself – what did I have to lose? Why not call? Mrs Buxton might know a neighbour or somewhere to live in the area.

Saved by a 'typo'. The notice should have read 'September'. I spent the next three years with Mrs Buxton, one of the kindest, most considerate and generous persons I have known. She opened her home to me. I had my own bedroom and living room and run of the house when she travelled, all for four pounds per week.

Recently widowed, Mrs Buxton found a new lease on life, traveling abroad with friends. Pointing to a huge cauldron of meat and vegetables: 'Elizabeth, do me a favour. I cooked all this food. I overlooked I am leaving for a few days. Please eat up – I would hate this to go to waste.'

Mrs Buxton held bridge card parties but made certain these did not coincide with my study times. She instructed all guests to remain quiet:

'Shh! My student is studying upstairs.' She banned her guests during exam times.

When she moved to another house nearby to join her brother and wife, I joined too as part of their family.

Mrs Buxton telephoned with pride her numerous friends and contacts when 'my (her) student' won the annual prize in orthopaedics. By coincidence, and no relation, the Buxton prize is named after St. John Dudley Buxton, founder of orthopaedic departments at several hospitals including King's College Hospital. When I qualified as a doctor in 1975, Mrs Buxton let the world know of 'my (her) student's' achievement. Three years later, as a Senior House Officer (SHO), I returned and stayed another six months while working at the London Chest Hospital in East London. Mrs Buxton made me feel at home. On reflection, this too was a first - my first untroubled home.

The Resolute Outsider

Chapter 9: How the **** did you get into medical school?

To a medical trainee, little compares to the thrill of arriving at a hospital to start clinical training – laying hands on patients. In the 1960s-1970s, during pre-clinical training in London - the first 18 months of medical school - students did not interact with patients. Instead, the curriculum focused on anatomy, physiology, biochemistry and pharmacology. The school deemed us fit to be let loose on patients only after passing the all-important second MB examination. Fortunately, in later decades, medical schools found wisdom to mix and match theory with clinical practice from the outset, much to the relief of would-be clinicians. Seeing patients and contributing to the advancement of society, however small, felt like a reward after three years learning minute details of the brachial plexus and Krebs' urea cycle. The year 1972 became the time to put hard-earned theory into practice.

On the outside, we resembled doctors. We dressed the same with the hallmark long white coat and stethoscope protruding proudly from a pocket. Draping this signature tool around the neck as a badge of honour became fashionable only decades later. However, the name badge (Mr, Miss) gave the game away. We were too young to be surgeons who prefer to be addressed as Mr, Mrs, or Ms rather than Dr. This custom dates back centuries when surgeons evolved from barbers who performed bloodletting among other invasive techniques without the requirement of a medical degree. Regardless, the glaring inexperience and fumbling when faced with a patient separated us amateurs easily from the professionals. We could recite the biochemistry of muscle metabolism but foundered on how to examine a patient.

In the 1970's women suffered transparent prejudice in the workplace and no less within the hallowed halls of medicine. Public opinion considered medicine a vocation, a calling, akin to becoming a priest or nun. However, many viewed women to be naturally devoid of these aspirations and not being up to the task. Those in charge of medical school admissions considered medicine as too stressful, too demanding and offered other epithets to justify our unsuitability. Worse, an undercurrent belief, albeit not spoken, held that a female medical student occupied a highly competitive seat better served by a (more deserving) male. Moreover, that coveted place would go to waste when she dropped out of medical school or clinical practice to do what women do: marry and care for children. Admissions staff overlooked a woman's natural ability to multitask. Determination and resolve carried little weight. That the British Government covered costs and living expenses completely during my training years, added justification for limiting the number of token places allocated to women. Government money should not be wasted. Despite data on women's longevity and achievements in medicine being comparable to men's, the prejudice against us remained all through the 1970's and for some time after I qualified (graduated) as a doctor (MB, BS) in the autumn of 1975.

Often on ward rounds as the lone female medical person, I would be relegated to the back behind a wall of enthusiastic male students vying for attention. Fortunately, few could ignore my height at 5ft. 11ins. (~180 cms). My voice, low-pitched for a female, carried above many heads into the ear of the instructor. With growing confidence and knowledge, I inched closer to the front. A consultant (attending) physician or surgeon on the ward took daily teaching rounds. Occasionally, an examiner in the medical school, who one day would judge a student's fitness to qualify and practice as a doctor, took these rounds.

That day came when the Vice Dean of the hospital took our student group – six males and me - on a teaching round. As a senior general surgeon and university examiner, he commanded equal portions of respect and attention. Surgery, even more than general medicine, was considered the exclusive bastion of men.

As expected, he directed all teaching questions to my male counterparts. The opportunity came after the Vice Dean fired a question at an adjacent student who remained silent. This was make or break time. The student hesitated. I did not and piped up, feeling pleased at knowing the answer. The silent student, relieved, nodded in agreement.

The Vice Dean pointed at me: 'You at the back, come to the front.' I smiled, believing he would commend my knowledge.

Instead, he frowned: 'What is your name? …. Ah, yes. How the **** did you get into medical school? You, a female, working class and you don't even play rugby!'

With a glare at the male students, he quashed their mumblings at his distain. A dismissal wave in my direction signalled to all his bias against women in medicine.

Raised in the army and with the nuns, I respected authority but the Vice Dean crossed a line. Plucking up courage, I stepped forward once more: 'I can add to the three negatives you list. I am left-handed, a Catholic and taller than most of the men here – all things you can stack against me but I will qualify and practice medicine, you shall see.' His steely eyes met mine in silence. His hand gestured for the ward round to continue. Summarily dismissed again.

Our session continued uneventfully but my male peers noted this event. I never disclosed personal challenges to classmates at the hospital. Regardless, they knew my resolve to become a doctor. At that time, being a woman attempting to succeed in a man's world garnered their admiration, regardless of additional baggage I might be carrying. Overall, the male medical students supported and respected us females. They acknowledged our focus and higher hoops we jumped through to enter medical school. Women, as a minority, gained a coveted place through attrition and tenacity coupled with arduous work. We added skills; a natural facility to multitask, show compassion and be a good listener – all considered 'soft' in my era. Only decades later these would be acknowledged as assets to enrich the profession. Meanwhile, many established members of the medical profession in the early 1970s failed to grasp the waves of change lapping at their doorsteps.

'The truth will out' is a lesson here. In 1983, I became an established physician on the staff at King's College Hospital Medical School and one of the few women pursuing a high-level medical career in gastroenterology and hepatology (liver disease). This senior surgeon, and former Vice Dean, sought me out. He remembered that teaching round from a decade before and acknowledged that I had 'stayed the course and done well.' We skirted around his former bias, now visibly an uncomfortable subject for him. He remained proud and projected that image. As a tall man, he walked upright with a silver cane and dressed in fine tailored suits with a cravat. He often spoke with pride of his brother, a high-ranking and well-known politician in Mrs Thatcher's Government.

The Vice Dean's negative attitudes towards women surprised me when I learned about his family history. His wife, now deceased, qualified as a doctor, and worked for years as a distinguished pathologist. He took pride in her pedigree coming from a titled medical family. Also, they had married young shortly after qualification. Ironically, on ward rounds he railed against medical students and newly qualified doctors marrying 'too young.'

Although never directly broaching the subject of his former bias against women in medicine and working-class folk, his actions spoke louder than words:

'Please meet me tomorrow morning for breakfast at 7.00AM in Piccadilly. This is not an invitation. This is a request and you will be glad you came.'

The following morning, after a short walk from our meeting point, we arrived at the door of a mansion. A butler showed us into a grand reception room with a high ceiling and several chandeliers. The former Vice Dean's brother, instantly recognizable from frequent appearances on the television and in the newspapers, came downstairs to greet us. I hope I hid my surprise. He wore a simple grey, cotton dressing gown over plain pajamas and bedroom slippers already down at the heel: 'I know all about you, come in and have breakfast. My wife will join shortly.'

For a brief time, they transported me into a different world and era of bygone days. Breakfast included Russian caviar on toast, kedgeree, and champagne with orange juice – rich man's buck fizz – at 7.30AM.

The brothers talked family business with occasional nods and smiles directed towards me. The famous brother turned towards me: 'Come with me, I wish to show you something.'

The butler escorted us into a library, the type seen in Hollywood films – oak paneled, books up to the beautifully corniced ceiling. More chandeliers. A large book lay open on a central lectern:

'Here is a first edition of Winston Churchill's writings, personally signed. I have just acquired this. You should read Churchill especially about his childhood days at Harrow – awfully entertaining.'

I remain struck by the paradox of a famous politician at ease in simple bedroom attire, munching toast and caviar and talking nonchalantly to me about Winston Churchill.

The former Vice Dean and I never discussed the purpose of my meeting his famous brother in such informal circumstances. By then, the former Vice Dean knew more about my background, by way of contrast with his, but our differences no longer mattered to him. I waited five more years to gain some insight. He continued to exhibit me to his distinguished family and inner circle of dignitaries, mostly in the arts. We visited Winchester College, his exclusive private boarding school in Hampshire. He enjoyed being identified as an 'Old Wykehamist'. I received a crash course in how the other half lives and speaks.

As his guest, along with another senior surgeon, the former Vice Dean took us to Glyndebourne opera to see Peter Grimes by Benjamin Britten. Now retired, the former Vice Dean spent his time at the opera, attending Ascot and mixing in exclusive circles with upper-class friends. On the outside, we remained worlds apart; however, he regularly sought me out to accompany him to the opera. He critiqued various performances as a newspaper columnist for the arts and ran drafts by me despite my limited knowledge. He favoured Verdi and Wagner and effused over outstanding performances; Nabucco at La Scala and several cycles of The Ring (Der Ring des Nibelungen) at home and abroad.

On a sunny day, in central London, en route to the Royal Opera House, we passed The Athenaeum, one of the few remaining private and exclusive clubs with male-only membership. The door attendant addressed the former Vice Dean by name and title and requested he collect a message inside.

I waved him on: 'I am happy to wait outside, go ahead and collect your message.'

'No', he replied, 'It is not gentlemanly to leave a lady standing at the doorstep. I do not understand why this club doesn't allow women inside.' Regardless of his response, I sensed reluctant acceptance to the openings becoming available to women when he added with a sigh: 'Afterall, we are in the 20th Century.'

As the years took their toll, he contacted me to oversee his general medical care when admitted increasingly frequently as a patient into our alma mater. By then, our worlds diverged further; mine, deep into work as a critical care hepatologist, on call 24/7 for liver transplantation and his, retired and ailing. His medical needs were outside of my field; however, he overruled attempts by his caring team for another doctor to intercede. His family reached out to me on his death, five years after our breakfast meeting in Piccadilly. They extended a personal invitation to the funeral.

Several hundred guests gathered in the grounds of the chapel and crematorium. Senior medical staff and former students mingled with dignitaries from the world of the arts. His famous brother, the politician, arrived shortly before the service began. Some luminaries circled around the Rolls Royce as the chauffeur drove into the centre of the grounds. After acknowledging them, his brother sought me out. We shared a few private words. He underscored my singular and lasting effect on his late brother. Above all, his late brother had been proud of me. What I became. What I overcame. We entered the chapel to the sung chorus of the Hebrew Slaves (Nabucco by Verdi).

Never underestimate the impact one can have. However, be prepared to wait, sometimes a decade, for any to be realised. When the former Vice Dean contacted me in 1983, I considered ignoring his requests to meet. On second thoughts, our meeting offered the opportunity to challenge his earlier negative attitudes towards women and working-class folk. I assumed naïvely that his biases and prejudices remained over the years. Instead, I realised we had matured. His subsequent actions in support of me and other medical students, spoke louder than words. Sometimes words are best left unspoken. In his waning years we shared an unwritten understanding. He knew that I knew that he knew of his former attitudes. In our mutual silence on the subject, he kept his pride; I maintained my dignity. Had I refused to meet again, I would have been deprived of our valuable and satisfying encounters.

In the UK and USA, starting around 2017, female medical students and doctors outnumber their male counterparts. In my era at King's, I am not aware of any female medical student dropping out during training because she could not cope or the training became too demanding. Women doctors who later left did so temporarily to raise a family or care for others. Facilities and support to help women balance a demanding career and family obligations were almost non-existent in the 1970s-1980s, even for the wealthy. To my knowledge, most women who qualify as doctors continue to practice regardless of raising a family or caring for other dependents. They are not lost. They return to the fold with more to give.

Chapter 10: Clinical training (1972 –1990); from blood to guts

King's College Hospital (KCH) remains one of the busiest teaching hospitals in London, even before the merger with St. Thomas' and Guy's occurring well after my time. During my clinical training years (1972-1975), KCH and the adjoining medical school (KCHMS) stood alone. Fortunately, clinical students had a high teacher-to-student ratio with plenty of patients to study. In between designated teaching rounds, lectures and practical sessions, student life revolved around clinics and Casualty (Emergency Department), where senior medical staff taught on a case-by-case basis. Medicine remains an apprenticeship, as in bygone days. A student learns at the hands (and more often feet) of the master – the consultant. We anchored reams of knowledge around individual patients – the case history. Thus, first steps began by clerking a patient – taking details of past and present illnesses. Most patients welcomed our interactions or at least accepted this intrusion as part and parcel of being in a teaching hospital.

The senior staff rewarded students staying late with one-on-one teaching on an 'interesting case of X disease.' Clinical medical school training consumed us in the 1970s. Life outside remained an afterthought.

On some rotations, we took turns to sleep in assigned students' accommodation in the terraced houses nearby. Long before the advent of mobile 'phones, we ran to the nearest land-line telephone when the pocket pager beeped. KCH in Denmark Hill, South London with its foundation stone laid there in 1909, displayed the Florence Nightingale style of wards in my time. Long corridors separated wards each with 20 to 40 parallel beds and a central nurses' station. Only a thin curtain separated each bed. Patients relinquished all sense of modesty and privacy as sound travelled around the ward: 'So how are the bowels today, Mrs.......?'

The days and months sped by as we rotated through the departments – cardiology, nephrology (kidney disease), respiratory diseases, obstetrics, gynaecology and more. My career track pointed towards haematology (blood disorders). I sowed the seeds of interest early as a phlebotomist and junior technician while studying at KCL and following a summer internship in Austria in 1971 (Chapter 8. 'King's College London (1969-1972); Medical school, firsts'). I enjoy the mix and match of clinical, working with patients and pathology – especially looking down the microscope. In the early 1970s serious blood disorders such as the leukaemias carried a poor prognosis. Fortunately, the speciality began to incorporate innovative technologies and treatments to improve patient outcomes. Riding the cusp of a new wave then and now appeals to me.

As the penultimate clinical year rolled around in 1974, I sought openings to spend the two months designated elective period in general medicine and especially infectious diseases, not a separate speciality at KCH. Unlike many peers who wanted to study near home, I chose to return to America. Emboldened from my summer internship at the Albert Einstein three years earlier, I applied to the Massachusetts General Hospital (MGH), the largest teaching hospital of Harvard University, in Boston. On my previous visit to the USA (1971), I worked exclusively in a laboratory far from patients. This time, I sought clinical experience.

Disappointment came early. From the vantage point of a student, the MGH contrasted sharply with KCHMS. The low ratio of instructors to students at MGH precluded informal teaching and direct examination of many patients. The attendings (consultants) at MGH taught us as afterthoughts. We hung around for crumbs of wisdom to fall off their tables. Unlike in the UK, American students, especially those able to afford the high university fees, could take time to graduate (qualify) as doctors. Several students studied part-time and repeated courses over years. Students selected fields of study and could graduate without setting foot in several key departments. I admired their air of confidence. They acknowledged my practical medical skills and ease at examining a patient despite our limited opportunities.

Given the high university tuition fees and expensive cost of living in Boston, students came mostly from privileged backgrounds – upper class by UK standards. They drove cars, lived in apartments, took holidays abroad and dined out in restaurants. Fortunately, no-one asked me about my background. In 1974, Americans judged a person on achievement, not pedigree. The students seemed content with limited access to examining patients directly despite being in a teaching hospital, but not me. In the 1970s, before the advent of the internet, desktop computers and remote learning, clinical training relied on being 'hands-on'- examining patients. Books came second best to palpating an enlarged spleen, auscultating (hearing) a heart murmur. Thus, I decided to switch to pathology. Although only a student, given my prior experience at KCH, the MGH granted wide access to materials and specimens.

The pathologists were grateful for an extra pair of hands. During my time, several members received letters from the Selective Service System, a branch of the US government involved with registration for the draft (compulsory military service) in readiness for war. Although the draft for the Vietnam war ended two years earlier, doctors of all specialities continued to be sought as reserve 'Medics' should hostilities resurface there or elsewhere. Pathologists, by nature, prefer to work behind the scenes. Several, including a senior neuropathologist, became conflicted at potentially being called up to serve 'at the front'. Thus, a silent cloud and collective Sword of Damocles hung over the department especially when anticipating a postal delivery of tell-tale brown, official-looking envelopes. They knew of my experiences living in conflict zones in Cyprus. I have not met a doctor or clinical medical student in favour of war.

In the remaining weeks at MGH, I became a prosector in anatomy and carried out post-mortems under the watchful eye of a senior pathologist. A prosector looks beyond the cause of death. We weighed, sampled and analysed under the microscope all organs and tissues of the body to build a data bank. The pathology department, through painstaking work, amassed information from head to toe, on the weight, size and structure of the pituitary gland, the prostate, the adrenal glands, and more. We demonstrated our findings to other anatomists in the department. In the early 1970s in America and the UK, teaching hospitals routinely conducted detailed post-mortems regardless of the known cause of death. At KCH, students spent many hours in the mortuary demonstration rooms poring over the prosector's findings, akin to a detective looking for unsuspected clues. By the 1990s, in the UK and USA, the numbers of post-mortems dwindled to all but a few unsolved cases. Rarely do people die in hospital without a pre-mortem diagnosis, given the advances in diagnostic techniques not available in my era.

As a student in Boston, I witnessed the underbelly of America. Admissions officers asked patients entering the Emergency Department for proof of health insurance before being examined by healthcare personnel. Staff searched unconscious patients for evidence of health coverage. They called an ambulance for uninsured patients who 'could make it' across the city to the State hospital accepting indigent patients. I admired much about America – the 'can do' attitude - but silently raged over the lack of a national healthcare safety net. I struggled then and now with the paradox that all men are created equal, stated in the American Constitution, but to paraphrase *Animal Farm* by George Orwell, *'some* (who can afford health insurance) *are more equal than others.'* The USA then, as now, is at the forefront of advances in medicine and science. I vowed if ever I returned to the USA as a doctor, I would work only in an Institution that provides for the poor and accommodates those without health insurance.

Thus, on return to KCHMS in the autumn of 1974, I prepared for the final exams (third and fourth MB, BS) to begin in the early summer of 1975. Also, I planned to sit the American Examination for Foreign Medical Graduates (ECFMG) soon after qualification while my exam-based knowledge was fresh. ECFMG certification, as an entry examination, would open the door to practice medicine in America. I envisaged spending a year at a renowned American Institution for higher speciality training to enhance my resumé back home.

Back to being a student, I happily completed the necessary rotations – all but two. Final year (senior) medical students rotated through the Liver Unit. KCH is world-famous for hepatology (liver diseases). Among many recognitions, KCH in partnership with Addenbrooke's Hospital, Cambridge, organised the first liver transplant in the UK in 1968. King's established the first paediatric liver unit in the world.

Despite international recognition, KCHMS students dreaded this rotation. In the 1970s, hepatology, as a medical speciality, was in its infancy with limited lay recognition and few treatment options available for patients. King's Liver Unit based on Todd Ward accepted only the sickest, most complex patients from around the world. The Unit specialised in acute liver failure – 'the fulminants'. Such patients often arrive unconscious, on death's door and require an army of medical and nursing staff trained in intensive care, including critical care hepatology. Many patients die waiting for a liver transplant. Patients with severe liver disorders are prone to bleeding, confusion, kidney failure, infections and more. The staff spend much time mopping up body fluids from the walls and floor while caring for disorientated patients. Those with viral hepatitis are potentially infectious, adding to the difficulties of their management and need to prevent spread of infection to all personnel in close contact. Few students contemplated a career in liver disease. In the 1970s, the higher training authorities did not recognise hepatology as a stand-alone specialty. Instead, would-be hepatologists practiced under the umbrella of gastroenterology without added recognition of this demanding sub-speciality. Accreditation in hepatology as a separate sub-speciality of gastroenterology, became available only decades later.

The notorious behaviour of the Liver Unit chief, Dr Roger Williams, -'RW' to insiders - added to the students' dread. RW had little time for junior staff, none for students and zero tolerance for female medical staff of all stripes. His towering frame projected a booming voice lambasting the latest victim of his ire well beyond the confines of Todd Ward.

Thus, I began the dreaded rotation on the Liver Unit. Senior staff counselled female students not to wear trousers (despite trouser suits being the fashion of the day) and to 'keep out of his way - be invisible,' unless addressed directly – an unlikely event given our lowly status.

An entourage of senior staff and visiting doctors from around the world accompanied Dr Williams on ward rounds. As instructed, we students melted into the background, ignominiously. The medical staff later explained any 'pearls of wisdom' expounded by the chief as he barrelled through the ward at breakneck speed. The staff assigned us menial tasks; drawing blood samples from patients, shunting them between Radiology and other departments and filling out paperwork. On rare occasions, Dr Williams acknowledged the presence of male students only to throw one into the deep end. With a penetrating glare and in full command of his tall frame, he barked: 'What is Mr X's haemoglobin level today?'

Doomed student: 'Erh, around twelve grams per litre, I think.'

Louder bark with added growl: 'What do you mean "around" and "you think?!" You should know the precise value!! That is not good enough. Leave the ward now and do not come back!!.....Next patient....'

We students felt sorry for the House Physicians (HPs) on the Liver Unit. KCH assigned three, rather than the typical two, HPs to 'The Firm' (Liver Unit) given the exacting demands of dealing with liver patients – and likely also the chief. Theirs was a thankless task spent running around day and night to manage extremely ill patients while placating the ever-demanding chief. We did not envy them.

Despite repeated humiliation at the hands of the chief, the three HPs remained kind and considerate to students. One HP, Peter Feltham, answered questions and softened the verbal blows raining down from on high. Peter maintained a wonderful sense of humour despite the daily barrage of demands and verbal onslaughts. Todd Ward functioned as a maternity ward prior to being transformed into the Liver Unit by Dr Williams. For years, letters arrived addressed to 'The De-Livery Unit'.

Many students counted down the hours to escape 'Liver', but not me. Liver diseases piqued my interest. I yearned for more. Nevertheless, we all looked forward to light relief in ear, nose and throat (ENT), the next assignment, positioned strategically to provide a reprieve from this predictable ordeal. The medical school added two days off in between to sleep and recoup. Students in the final year did not take holidays.

With less than one week to go 'on Liver', I joined the early morning ward round. We students banded together for emotional support behind a wall of visiting dignitaries crowding around Dr Williams. Immediately I noticed the absence of the housemen.

As usual, Dr Williams started barking orders to anyone within earshot: 'I want.... where is.... why hasn't this been done......?'

Dr Hugh Tubbs, the Senior Registrar and right-hand man on the Unit, piped up: 'Peter, the HP, is ill. We admitted him to hospital yesterday. The other HPs are trying to catch up. We urgently need someone to cover Peter's duties.'

More booming from the chief: 'Well, for goodness sakes, get someone. I need the results now,' and off he stormed.

The Senior Registrar turned to us students huddled at the back of the entourage. This commanding physician, as tall as RW, but absent the boom, called me to come forward: 'Would you be willing to be "shadow" houseman?'

Excited to be singled out to work as a 'real' doctor but reluctant to lose out on my general training, I deflected: 'Um, I am due to go on to ENT next week.'

'Oh, don't worry, we can fix that.'

'But I am only a student.'

Pointing to an army of Liver Unit doctors from the research unit above Todd Ward, Dr Tubbs continued: 'We know. We will supervise and cover you. After all, the HP spends most of his time doing administrative stuff. You start now. I will let RW know.'

Dr Tubbs handed me Peter's pager and keys to a room in the hospital wing where house staff slept. On our one-on-one ward round, I learnt more in one hour than in four weeks. Armed with a laundry list of tasks, I set to and recited: 'Take the patient in bed five to Radiology. Repeat blood tests on bed seven'...... and so on.

The days and nights are a blur. I do not recall using the allocated hospital room. HPs on the Liver Unit had no official days off. The HPs and I passed as ships in the night, except at full throttle speeding to our next emergency call, and in our minds silently calling out *Mayday, Mayday*. Each Firm, including the Liver Unit, took turns to cover Casualty over weekends – admitting emergency general medicine patients – while also working on Todd Ward. The unwritten rule, based on the severity of illnesses and preference of the chief, stated that Todd Ward be reserved exclusively for liver patients. Accordingly, we admitted general medical patients on 'Take' weekends to all wards except the Liver Unit. This arrangement added miles of corridors to cover. Junior staff cared for general medical patients scattered across the length and breadth of our large, sprawling hospital while running back and forth to Todd Ward. Moreover, Casualty, located at the other end of the hospital from Todd Ward, required an extra sprint when the emergency admissions' pager summoned.

After one of those four-day weekends covering Casualty and running between multiple wards and the Liver Unit, I joined Dr Williams starting his Monday morning ward round. A larger than usual entourage of visiting dignitaries crowded around the chief. Relegated to the back of the group as befitted my student badge, thoughts turned to food, a shower, a change clothes and, above all, sleep.

Dr Williams in fine fettle continued his usual tirade: 'Where are the results for bed eight? I want...., where is that houseman – why isn't he here?'

I piped up from behind the crowd: 'I am here, the student, covering for Dr Peter....'

RW did not acknowledge my presence. He continued to shout over the heads of visiting professors: 'What did the ascites (belly fluid) tap show for bed six.... where are the lumbar puncture results, why hasn't.....?'

I had had enough. Mustering residual strength despite fatigue, a rumbling empty stomach and sleep deprivation, I raised my voice to carry over the multiple heads between me and the chief: 'Don't shout at me. I am only a student. I am not allowed to tap ascites and do lumbar punctures. I am doing my level best.'

I interpreted the ensuing silence in the room as a death knell sounding loudly against my aspirations to qualify as a doctor within a year. From his towering height, RW glared in my direction over the visiting heads. The entourage made way – parting of the Red Sea comes to mind – and faded into the background as RW strode towards me.

Suddenly, with a change in demeanour, he looked down on me, lowered his voice and spoke quietly as we came face-to-face: 'What do you think of me?'

I had his attention. My time to boom: 'I think you are a prize rat!' I mopped tears away with my coat sleeve, believing this expletive sabotaged my future. Impertinence warranted a reprimand from the medical training hierarchy and likely banishment from the Liver Unit.

RW ignored the gasps of consternation from the crowd. His smile and nod prompted me to continue: 'You want tomorrow's results yesterday. I am only a student, volunteering to help. All you do is shout orders at the HPs. I am not qualified to carry out the procedures you want done.'

With this additional outpouring, I envisaged a likely complaint for insolence filed with the medical school Dean and dismissal from KCHMS. No going back. I had nothing to lose. I had sabotaged all chances of remaining at King's to complete my training despite a yearning to learn. This outburst put my future on the line. I took a deep breath. 'I want to....'

'What do you want?'

'I want to learn about liver disease. All I do is rush around filling forms, drawing blood and pushing patients to Radiology.'

'Alright. I will teach you liver disease. Meet me every Friday, four o'clock in the private wing.'

And with that final remark, we moved on and finished the ward round. No further demands. No reprimands. No black marks filed against me.

Thereafter, the medical and nursing staff treated me differently: 'Wow, you had the guts to stand up to RW.' I became part of their team. Under strict supervision, they allowed me to perform lumbar punctures, liver biopsies and drain ascites.

Dr Williams kept his word. The private wing of the hospital excluded students. He circumvented this rule with my designation as 'shadow HP.' He taught me one-on-one long after I moved beyond the Liver Unit. Private patients came from abroad with a breath-taking constellation of diverse, often exotic, liver diseases. RW demonstrated their signs and symptoms and allowed me to examine them, as the 'shadow HP.' I learned a different side to this great man. What he lacked in quiet bedside manner, he surpassed in diagnostic skills, brilliance and acumen for his craft. Without the invention of CT scans and MRIs, many diagnoses came from the laying on of hands - physical examination of the patient - and liver biopsy. Often the patient did not speak English and outside hospital records gave no direction of a diagnosis. Patients reached King's after weeks and months of tests and several opinions from primary and secondary referring hospitals. I witnessed RW diagnose patients within minutes of their entering the room and standing before him – no need to sit down; a chair was not provided.

In 1975 as the final exams loomed, senior medical students applied for house jobs; HP or House Surgeon (HS). Unlike the USA, the medical degree in the UK is undergraduate – a bachelor's degree in Medicine

(MB) and Surgery (BS or BCh). To that end, the first twelve months after graduation in the UK are considered provisional qualifications, with the courtesy title of 'doctor.' Long after my era, this first year became designated as a Foundation (F1) year. The newly qualified 'doctor' spends that provisional year equally divided between medical (HP) and surgical (HS) posts before being approved ('licensed') by the General Medical Council (GMC) to practice medicine – a fully qualified doctor. Despite the notoriety of the Liver Unit and its chief, many students sought the three HP posts, given the prestige and opportunity to work in a world-renowned department. Rationale followed that this trial by fire upheld Darwin's Law – the fittest will survive on subsequent posts. Roger Williams had his pick of the top students.

I applied for the HP job on the Liver Unit, believing this would go to the future gold medallist or top student of the day. I placed well in the final MB, BS with two honour-level *viva voce* (oral) examinations in pathology and obstetrics but several students surpassed me.

The day I received my MB, BS results from the Dean's office, this newly minted doctor headed straight to the airport, suitcase in hand. Over several years, and thanks to Mrs Buxton's generosity, I saved the airfare (730 pounds sterling in 1975 – more than a year's government grant allowance) for a flight to New Zealand to see my sister, Mary. I missed her wedding in 1973 and the recent birth of her firstborn daughter. At least I would be there for the baptism.

My sister had settled in a rural part of the North Island of New Zealand. The mail arrived intermittently by water 'plane. We walked to the nearby estuary every few days to collect the post.

By blue aerogram letter: *'We are pleased to inform you that you have been accepted as House Physician to Roger Williams on the Liver Unit. You start 01 January 1976.'* In custom of the day the pre-registration appointments of HP and HS came without notification of salary. We assumed we would be paid – and we were - the princely sum of 2,100 pounds per annum. In 2022, allowing for inflation, this equates to under 20,000 pounds.

This starting date is etched in my mind as well as King's. Due to flight delays, I arrived in London late on New Year's Eve. The next day, 01 January 1976, started with a bang, minimal sleep and jet lag. I witnessed the first liver transplant to be carried out at KCH, rather than Addenbrooke's Hospital, Cambridge. Despite our rudimentary understanding of transplant immunology and cellular rejection the patient recovered, becoming one of the longest survivors of the UK transplant program.

The six-month post on the Liver Unit flew by but the thrill of being at the frontier of medicine remains a treasured memory. A designated Liver Failure Unit (LFU) elevated the King's Liver Unit to world-class status in this field. In the 1970s-1980s, King's accepted 50-100 'fulminants' (acute liver failure) patients a year to the two-bed LFU supported by a legion of dedicated staff. Caring for the fulminants and liver transplant patients is the pinnacle of achievement for hepatology. Although the most junior of the medical team with limited skills and minimal practical experience, I realised within days of starting as a doctor that I wanted to be not only a hepatologist but also a critical care hepatologist. The medical, nursing and technical staff work as a team. Hierarchies are forgotten when faced with desperately ill patients – all hands to the deck. I never heard 'that is not my job' if I, the most junior 'medic' around, asked a senior physician to run to the blood bank for more blood supplies. We set aside political differences and personal disagreements as the team together battled to replace litres of blood pouring out of a patient haemorrhaging before our eyes. Cerebral oedema (brain swelling) is a life-threatening complication of acute liver failure and requires around-the-clock monitoring and judicious use of medications such as mannitol. The Liver Unit strived to be self-sufficient. We hepatologists became expert in the management of cerebral oedema, usually the remit of neurologists. As a team we supported each other when we lost a patient. Equally we rejoiced as one when a 'fulminant' awoke from a coma or when a patient could be weaned off life support. Dr Williams continued to demand 'tomorrow's results, yesterday' interspersed with pearls of wisdom from his unrivalled experience and expertise in hepatology.

True to form, working on the Liver Unit opened many doors. I went on to a top HS post, also at King's. In 1977, now a fully qualified doctor according to the GMC, I successfully interviewed for gastroenterology as Senior House Officer (SHO) on the Professorial Unit at the Hammersmith Hospital with its Royal Postgraduate Medical School (RPMS).

Successive panels of interviewers over the years noted I had 'survived' *the* (King's) Liver Unit. Further top SHO posts followed on the Professorial Units at Royal Brompton and the London Chest Hospital. Thereafter, I returned to the Hammersmith Hospital in 1979 as a Registrar and research fellow in gastroenterology and general medicine.

In 1983, I wrote to Dr Williams for a reference to pursue gastroenterology further in Cambridge. His secretary telephoned me: 'RW refuses your request. He orders you to come to King's this week for an explanation.' I requested time off to make the train and bus journey back to South London. Annoyed by his negative response, I could see no reason for Dr Williams to refuse my request. In my eyes, I had several accomplishments under my belt despite overcoming recent health challenges (Chapters 11-14). In 1982, I completed with Distinction a Master of Science (MSc) in immunology at Chelsea College, later merging with King's. Also, the New England Journal of Medicine recently accepted a paper on lung and liver disease with me, as first author from my time at Royal Brompton – no mean feat for a mid-level physician (Registrar), and a Brit at that.

No longer intimidated, I walked confidently into his office and came straight to the point: 'Why will you not give me a reference? Do you remember me? You wrote thanking me for great work as an HP back in 1976. What did I do wrong?'

Again, that wry smile I recognised from years back: 'Of course I remember you. You called me a prize rat!'

No bark. More of a rumble as he continued: 'You need to return to King's and work for me. I can offer you a Senior Registrar post. Your place is in hepatology and at King's.'

'But hepatology is not even recognized as a speciality. I need recognition in gastroenterology.'

'You can get your gastroenterology recognition working for me. I will see to that. King's is your home.'

And so, I returned to the Liver Unit in 1983 as a Senior Registrar in general medicine and gastroenterology (hepatology). My specialty training took a further seven years to be recognized. In November 1990, the newly formed Joint Commission on Higher Medical Training (JCHMT) issued their diploma to recognize completion of my training in internal medicine and gastroenterology, but only dating from 1990. By then I had notched up more than 14 years' experience in general medicine and 11 years in gastroenterology and hepatology. I held a unique tenured post as a Lecturer in hepatology on the Liver Unit.

In January 1991, I moved to the Royal Free Hospital School of Medicine (RFHSM) – the other institution in London famous for liver disease with added facilities in advanced molecular virology. I transferred as a full-time virologist and Senior Research Fellow with a Wellcome Fellowship grant to work on candidate hepatitis F, a potentially novel virus found in acute liver failure of unknown cause. Few doctors and scientists moved between the two liver institutions such was their loyalty to respective mentors and faculty. Some colleagues regarded my move to the RFHSM as being disloyal to King's and RW. Others acknowledged my resolve to pursue a project that would likely delay my clinical career advancement. During my first week at the RFHSM, Dr Williams arrived there unannounced much to the consternation of the staff and scientists as he boomed: 'Where is Dr Fagan?'

On finding me gowned in protective gear with test tubes and pipette in hand, RW lowered his voice: 'Ah, good. Just here to see you are settling in.' He admitted he had not set foot in the hepatology department in over 20 years since training at the RFHSM under Professor Sheila Sherlock – the founder of Hepatology in the UK.

Dr Williams, later Professor, kept in touch throughout my training and postgraduate undertakings over 45 years. Our plans to meet again in April 2020 were foiled by travel restrictions imposed by the SARS-CoV-2 pandemic. He died from unrelated causes in July 2020.

The winding path to my final choice of career from possible haematologist to happy gastroenterologist and hepatologist illustrates how the winds of change can steer an unexpected course.

Why did I choose hepatology? There is no single answer. My career began before patients with liver disease had many options for treatment. Then, few doctors in general medicine had in-depth knowledge of hepatology although deaths due to liver diseases are higher than for kidney disease, hypertension, colorectal cancer or breast cancer according to World Health rankings. Moreover, in my era some regarded liver patients as 'lepers', being potentially infectious, complicated and difficult to manage. Patients with advanced liver disease can bleed copiously, vomit and develop diarrhoea, confusion and more. This messy side of medicine rarely is conveyed via television, theatre performances and on the silver screen. Instead, the public typically is offered a sanitised and glamourised perspective of life on a hospital ward. Girls wishing to study medicine not uncommonly voice their future career aspirations to be in paediatrics or obstetrics. However, reality often sets in regarding a doctor's limitation to cure when faced with a suffering child or a dying baby. For me, I entered medicine without any illusions about 'saving lives' (Chapter 1. So you want to be a doctor?'). I prefer to work with the seriously ill, knowing that the odds of their survival can be low. Many patients with advanced liver disease require critical care (Intensive care unit (ICU)) support. Patients with acute liver failure - the fulminants - require a 24/7 commitment from a dedicated team of highly trained doctors, nurses, and technical support. King's pioneered their care. I am a witness.

My journey coincided with the advent of innovative technologies and interventions. Experts from around the world came to King's to train in liver disease. I witnessed the revolution of a discipline within my own backyard and many 'firsts' during the early years. As mentioned earlier, the first liver transplant at KCH occurred on New Year's Day, 1976 - my first day as a doctor. In 1983, within days of returning to King's after a seven-year interval to train in gastroenterology, cardiology and respiratory medicine, I cared for the first paediatric liver transplant recipient in the UK. Safe and effective vaccines became available for hepatitis B – an infection that kills millions every year from chronic liver disease and liver cancer. In 1988, I embarked on an around-the-world tour to raise awareness of immunisation against hepatitis B virus, an important cause of liver cancer. Hepatitis B vaccine can be regarded as the first anti-cancer vaccine. Scientists in America discovered hepatitis C virus and developed an assay to diagnose the infection in 1989. Great advances continued in autoimmune hepatitis and control of bleeding, infection and other complications common in advanced liver disease. Surgery for paediatric liver diseases advanced dramatically. The survival rate of a fulminant, below 50 per cent when I started on the Liver Failure Unit in 1983, improved progressively. Seven years later, in 1991 when I moved on, survival rates were much higher, depending on the underlying cause and expanding availability of liver donation and liver transplantation.

Students and junior doctors in more recent times have asked: 'Why did you put up with the endless hours (no shifts) as a clinical student and junior doctor?'

The simple answer is: 'We did not know any different.'

In the 1970s, medical students and junior doctors worked until the patients were stable – a rare occurrence. Junior doctors on the Liver Unit worked a 1-in-2 rotation - every second weekend off – except not off completely. A weekend 'off ' meant attending the Saturday morning three-hour tutorial round held by RW. All medical staff attended. Sunday afternoon 'off' meant clerking (admitting) all complex patients for the week ahead. On a weekend 'off' I slept Saturday afternoon through to Sunday morning and woke to complete my laundry before returning to the patients. All outside activities focused on surviving the two weeks ahead. The ensuing weekend on duty, meant working non-stop, around the clock, from Friday morning through Monday evening. I rarely took off my shoes. Non-medical friends and family exclaimed: 'But, you had no other life, no family of your own, no fun, no holidays.... all that studying... working more than 80 hours a week.... that must have been miserable........ and you were paid a pittance with no overtime.'

In my era, few junior medical colleagues married or had long-term stable relationships. I felt sorry for any shouldering these added responsibilities. For me, I exhausted all personal reserves beyond the bounds of work. I had an added reason for being a social outsider – a Sword of Damocles hung over me (Chapters 11 and 12).

My response to the endless cycle of work-sleep-work is simple: 'We accepted this life.' Without false modesty, this is the price we paid. No doubt in my era, junior doctors and nurses, as the workhorses of the profession, were taken for granted. The assumption that saving lives alone was sufficient reward for all our training and personal sacrifice overlooked saving our own lives and health. On a per hour rata, we were paid less than many unskilled workers. Junior doctors forged their own career paths with little guidance from the hierarchy. Within medicine in the UK, certification as a specialist was unstructured. No number of years served in the field guaranteed recognition or promotion. Attaining a consultancy and especially an academic appointment, such as professor, relied on 'dead men's shoes', despite proficiency. Regardless, I view medicine as a vocation and a lifelong apprenticeship - a throwback to earlier centuries of medical clerks and barbers. Medicine is one of the few professions where grey hair is viewed as an asset. I knew how to be a doctor until the day I qualified. Since then, I remain a student.

Chapter 11: Physician, heal thyself*

Medice, cura te ipsum; Luke 4:23:

*You have suffered sorrow and humiliation. You have lost your wits and have gone astray; and, like an unskilled doctor, fallen ill, you lose heart and cannot discover by which remedies to cure your own disease. From *Prometheus Bound* attributed to Aeschylus (~525-455 BC).

Upon reflection, the headaches began around 14 years of age. Our general practitioner attributed their onset and frequency to stress within our dysfunctional home, typical 'growing pains' and angst from being a lanky and awkward teenager facing high-school examinations. As the years passed, the headaches established a pattern of monthly cycles lasting up to four days, relieved in part by simple analgesics and sleeping them off.

After several futile attempts in the 1970s during medical school using simple tests and exploratory surgeries for corresponding gynaecological issues, the diagnosis remained elusive. The caring physicians and surgeons seemed content to attribute their gradual worsening to the demands of medical school and, later, to being a junior doctor: 'All will get better once you have established yourself in a career and settled down.'

'Take life easier' - if not easy, became the mantra. I resolved never to use that phrase glibly with patients.

Thus far, the symptoms had not interfered with high school, medical school, my clinical performance and medical career aspirations. In truth, I refused to let them interfere with these milestones. Throughout, I kept secret any hint of illness and took pride in my resolve. I never took one day off for illness in medical school or during any rotation since qualifying as a doctor. I timed investigations strategically to coincide with weekends, holidays and between jobs. Underneath this layer of pride loomed fear of losing my place on the ladder of a medical career – or worse, being denied a footing. Why would any hospital or medical practice hire me? I competed for top positions with able-bodied doctors holding stellar credentials. Worse still, I was a woman, and with an undiagnosed illness. And an unknown prognosis.

In the 1970s-1980s, some peers viewed as inadequate those who 'dropped out' from medicine, regardless of cause. He, or when she, 'couldn't hack it'. Guilt followed especially for women who 'wasted' their medical training to leave and raise a family. That slot should have gone to a man. Worse, anyone attempting to return to medicine after a 'time out' found their career ladder became steeper.

In the UK, the General Medical Council (GMC) governs fitness to practice but provided no sound guidance in the 1970s for doctors with disability or chronic illness. Outwardly I showed no disability - no wheelchair, crutches or white stick to evoke sympathy or visible understanding of need. The UK Government issued the Disability Discrimination Act to accommodate disabled and chronically ill individuals at work in 1995 - 20 years after I qualified as a doctor.

Although initially reassured by all the negative tests - 'all clear' - the lack of a diagnosis loomed. Throughout, I remained resolute to become an accomplished physician-scientist come hell or high water. I never contemplated an alternative career. I placed all those eggs in one basket a long time ago. Any social life took a back seat. My basket was full leaving no room for more uncertainties. No doubt some colleagues thought me odd, even anti-social. Others intimated that I must be hiding 'in the closet' - a phrase used indirectly in the 1970s for gay and other marginalised people. I preferred to be misrepresented at the price of keeping secret my health challenges.

By mid 1977, around eighteen months after qualifying as a doctor, my career trajectory looked bright. I passed the Membership of the Royal College of Physicians' (MRCP) Part I examination first time around. That milestone is regarded as a first large step up the ladder to an academic medical career. Despite a commitment to becoming a gastroenterologist, I competed successfully for the top junior post (Senior House Officer: SHO) on the Professorial Unit at Royal Brompton Hospital, renowned for diseases of the lungs and heart. I purposely sought out training in chest medicine given the high frequency of lung disease in the general population. In the 1970s many people smoked, including medical personnel. I am a life-long non-smoker, despite being raised in a household filled with second-hand smoke. In between the long and tiring days, I continued to browse the medical literature relating to obscure headaches. This era predated advanced radiological imaging techniques such as CT-scans and magnetic resonance Imaging (MRI).

No news can be more difficult to handle than bad news. I managed the uncertainty of my diagnosis the only way I knew: to work hard and bury myself in the misery of others. At 27 years of age, several friends and peers had moved on with their lives, now they had a life outside of medicine. They reaped the personal rewards following years of study, hard work and dedication to others. Several settled down. Some planted roots and joined a general practice or speciality providing stability in location and earnings. I rejoiced in their weddings and partnerships, the births of their children, adoption of pets and other happy occasions.

The rotation at Royal Brompton included three months secondment to the original Frimley Park Hospital, a satellite branch in the countryside, 40 miles west of London. This former sanatorium for tuberculosis (TB), opened in 1905 and closed in 2014. This old hospital offered respite from the hectic pace of London. The building is designed as a cross. The four main wings and wards face south onto spectacular views. Patients took in the air with graded exercises in the grounds, a treatment considered beneficial for TB patients at the turn of the 20th century. In my time, Brompton in London sent heart and lung patients to convalesce amid beautiful grounds with trees, flowers and abundant wildlife. In hindsight, this rotation became a personal blessing. The slower pace meant I could catch up with sleep and take time to think and prioritise my health. As in high school (Chapter 3. 'Beware - do not feed; this specimen is rare.'), I spent hours in the library alone perusing books, and journals – this time all medical and looking for rare diseases. My fellow Senior House Officer preferred to explore the grounds. I hunted for a diagnosis.

On free weekends, a welcome respite, I returned to London to scour medical publications in the large libraries of London University but drew only blanks. Finally, in late 1977, a solitary paper recently published described a small number of patients with headaches and gynaecological issues like mine attributed to an enlarged pituitary, an endocrine (hormone) gland situated deep in the middle of the head. This condition is associated with elevated levels of the hormone prolactin. In my mind, testing for this uncommon condition seemed worth a shot having exhausted the list of many causes of headaches in a young woman. I sent into the local laboratory under a pseudonym for a hypothetical patient, a blood sample for a prolactin level. Not for one moment did I expect the test result to be anything else but within the normal range. The ward rounds, night-calls and headaches continued.

Two weeks later, the local laboratory director interrupted a ward round exclaiming excitedly: 'Dr Fagan, you are not going to believe this! Your patient has the most amazingly elevated levels of prolactin I have ever seen – in fact, we sent her blood test out to our regional lab to make sure we hadn't made a mistake, but we hadn't. The sample had to be diluted because her levels were "off the chart! "'

Feigning composure: 'Thank you for the result…. I will discuss this with… uh… the patient.'

'Well, let us know what happens to her and if she needs a follow-up test – great to have an odd case. Keeps us interested and on our toes.'

I made some excuse to leave the ward round and find a quiet space. Ironically, I felt calm and at peace with being odd once more. At last, after more than a decade of tests and living with the unknown, I had a diagnosis – prolactinoma. As soon as the ward round finished, I raced to the library to find out more. In 1977, the scanty literature offered little, especially in a hospital dedicated to lung and heart diseases. These days preceded the internet.

Over time, I discovered most prolactinomas are benign (not cancer). I convinced myself my tumour must be benign too. I had this for more than a decade, based on symptoms, which is not the typical path for malignant brain tumours. I faced a major hurdle to disclose this illness to my superiors. And with that, all the uncertainties about the future flooded back. The truth will out.

The professors showed concern; however, they focused on my completing the nine-month rotation. With three months left, I agreed to continue working, having waited 13-plus years. Meanwhile, I put on hold all searches for the next post. Ahead loomed the final (Part II) MRCP, a practical and written examination and essential rite of passage for physicians with high academic career aspirations.

As soon as my rotation returned to the Royal Brompton in London, I referred myself to Professor John Nabarro, a noted endocrinologist at the Middlesex hospital in central London. Repeat blood testing showed the prolactin levels were higher than before. In the 1970s, without available medications, pituitary surgery, a risky procedure, offered the only hope of controlling the condition. The pituitary, the master endocrine (hormone) gland, produces at least six hormones, apart from prolactin, and controls other endocrine glands (thyroid, adrenals, ovaries). Simply, the pituitary gland products interact with many parts of the body, from control of fluids via antidiuretic hormone (ADH) on the kidney, to control of skin, bone, the reproductive system and more. The pituitary is difficult to reach even with advanced stereotactic equipment not available in the 1970s. This gland, located deep inside the head, sits below the optic (eye) nerves and links with the brain via a critical connection, the hypothalamus. Removing too much pituitary relegates the patient to a lifetime of tests, close medical monitoring, and prescriptions of a complex cocktail of hormones to replace those no longer produced or controlled by the deficient gland.

In the 1970s, few surgeons in the UK operated on pituitary tumours. Coincidentally, Mr Williams, an Ear, Nose and Throat (ENT) surgeon also worked at the Middlesex Hospital. He had years of experience at trans-sphenoidal hypophysectomy – removing other types of pituitary tumours via the nose and face. In 1977, only simple radiographs were available to image inside the head. My few regular days off were consumed with tests to determine operability of the tumour. Plain X-rays of the head showed an expanded sella turcica – the cavity seat for the pituitary gland; however, the surgical team needed to define any upward expansion for their surgical approach via the nose or brain. I surprised the few people who knew about my situation by remaining calm as I waited many weeks for a decision on surgery and operability:

'You seem to be taking all this remarkably well. I am not sure I would be so calm in your shoes.'

'I have no choice.'

'Yes, but you are facing major "brain" surgery – aren't you even a bit nervous?'

'I have no choice. This is not going away. I have waited half my life for a diagnosis. There are no other options.'

Work continued uninterrupted with days and nights on call. In fact, work became the antidote to fears and uncertainty about my future.

I dreaded breaking the news to mother. By then, she had left Bath and worked as a housekeeper to a wealthy family in Lane End, a small village in Buckinghamshire, 50 kilometres (30 miles), outside of London. Not surprisingly, she was devastated. The shining lights in mother's life were her two daughters. Our successes gave her pride. Mother lived her dreams and aspirations through us. Her struggles continued these eight years since abandoning the home. Although recently she became more secure with a two-room suite, an improved weekly wage and considerate employers, the emotional toll of a failed marriage, being a divorcée and starting over in life beyond 50 years of age continued to weigh heavily. As time passed, the sparkle in her demeanour faded as did signs of her once extrovert, fun-loving, personality. She resigned herself to life as a cleaner or other subservient role and considered her future 'helpless and hopeless' - labels voiced decades before by her ex-husband and our father. Throughout her marriage, he called her stupid, ignorant, worthless, and useless. Those descriptions stuck despite my protestations over many years. Once more, she felt useless and doubly helpless as I tried to explain my health situation. In her eyes I remained her youngest child. She could not help, only worry.

Worse, mother had no family support system. Her only other relative in contact, her oldest daughter, lived half a world away. My sister Mary, a highly qualified nurse, emigrated to New Zealand in 1972, married and settled into raising a young family. We stayed connected albeit infrequently. This era predated emails, social media and web-based platforms to bridge the 11-hour time difference with the UK. Blue aerogram letters took three weeks each way. We agreed not to worry Mary over the troubling details and uncertainties given the distance and priorities of her raising two small children.

I timed detailed investigations to start after I finished at the Brompton. My track record of completing the jobs with no time off for illness remained; however, this came at a price. I had no income. I embarked on my own medical journey and unknown future while unemployed and unemployable. Over the years, I diligently accumulated some savings for a 'rainy day' but faced a potential monsoon with no other financial well on which to draw. I shared a flat and household expenses with Maureen, another 'Bromptonian' SHO, who paid more than her share, but soon she had to move on as junior doctors do.

No senior or supervisor from my circle at work who knew my circumstances offered practical or financial advice and support, a price for being fiercely independent. I say that without bitterness. No doubt help would have been offered had I asked. Our family circumstances conditioned me to never ask for help. Our military background loomed large; anything less than 'soldiering on' would display weakness. Also, I repeatedly asked only immediate supervisors from work be given details of my medical predicament. None of that inner circle at work or the medical staff looking after me asked about personal circumstances; how to manage financially and emotionally. Through no one else's fault, I faced these hardships alone – a family trait as an outsider.

When asked about the worst experience from those dark days before surgery, without hesitation, I recall the detailed testing to determine operability based on the size and extent of the tumour. I would not wish an air encephalogram on my worst enemy. Fortunately, in recent decades, non-invasive imaging (CT, MRI) replaced this barbaric, albeit useful, technique in its day. Under general anaesthesia, air is introduced into the brain via the spinal canal. The initial procedure resembles a lumbar puncture, except air is deliberately introduced into the brain cavities (ventricles) via the spinal canal. The X-ray pictures rely on contrasting densities of air, bone and brain. I woke up in the hospital ward with the cot sides of the bed raised and padded 'for your own protection.' A blindfold obscured light to lessen headache. At that time, the typical hospital ward in London teaching hospitals, including King's and the Middlesex, had 20 to 40 beds aligned in rows on either side of a central nurses' station. Noises carried around the ward. Lights remained on at night since patients required 24-hour attention. The ward knew from the moaning, restlessness and thrashing around which patient had undergone an air encephalogram.

'You may experience a bit of a headache afterwards,' is an understatement. These new headaches, although different, were relentless and superimposed on the original ones. Partial relief came from lying down on my left side. Painkillers of all stripes failed to lessen the throbbing sensation in my head. For the first few days, I remained bed bound. Any attempt to sit up resulted in significant worsening of the headaches – old and new. I ate while lying down. Drinking tea required a long straw.

Life on the ward revolved around the rounds by the surgeons. Despite protests to leave me be, the nurses fussed to ensure all beds were freshly made, flower vases refreshed and bedside tables cleaned and decluttered. Mr Williams, the ENT surgeon, beamed a smile my way as I lifted the blindfold a few seconds: 'We have some good news. Your tumour seems operable from the nose. No need to open the skull. However, there are no guarantees of success.'

I experienced first-hand how patients hang on to every thread of good news and blot out any bad. The 'However….' is a distant memory. Despite my medical background, as the patient, I struggled to make sense of the jargon in an unfamiliar medical field amid the fog of debilitating headaches. Ironically, as a medical student, I missed only one training rotation - ENT- due to covering the Liver Unit at King's as shadow houseman. Was this punishment from the Gods?

Meanwhile, I needed to fall back on something positive in my life. As a student, I took pride in an unbroken record of passing all tests and exams, starting after the 11-plus exam 15 years before (Chapter 1. 'So, you want to be a doctor?'). Resolute as ever, soon after discharge from hospital, I took the MRCP Part II written and practical exams. I curtailed a physical examination on a patient I considered too ill to take part. He needed medical attention by caring physicians, not being poked and prodded by exam candidates. With no surprise, I received a notice from the examination authorities to re-sit the patient examination section again.

The surgeons booked the pituitary operation for the 14th of April 1978, two weeks after I completed the Brompton rotation. Meanwhile, I needed distraction and, once more, resorted to the only way I knew how. After a few days to put my house and financial affairs in order, as before, I buried myself in work. I took a locum (temporary) job at Watford General Hospital, a busy suburban hospital near London. My old feelings of financial insecurity resurfaced again. I needed a financial safety net for the unknown duration of time off work following surgery and rehabilitation.

At no time did I contemplate an end to my medical career. Regardless of the many uncertainties surrounding any future ability to work, medicine or not, my focus remained on re-joining the precarious and steep climb within academic medicine. Gastroenterology, which included hepatology in the 1970s, remains a competitive and demanding speciality. The practical aspects, for example, endoscopy and biopsy, especially appeal to me. These procedures require stamina and focus when handling equipment, standing in operating rooms and dealing with extremely ill and complex patients. Despite these challenges, I viewed gastroenterology as my 'best shot', having a foothold and recognition within the speciality, albeit at junior level.

The temporary post at Watford General Hospital over the weekend before my operation altered my decision to pursue immediately gastroenterology. At Watford, as the on-call general house physician, I accepted emergency patients through the Casualty Department. I shared an instant rapport with the supervisor, an established gastroenterologist, given our common interest.

The emergency pager summoned me to the Casualty Department. A young pregnant woman arriving by ambulance experienced fainting attacks. Her pulse rate was 40 beats per minute – almost half the normal rate. The electrocardiogram (ECG) showed heart-block. I knew enough cardiology to recognize heart block can occur in pregnancy. Importantly, she needed a pacemaker, *statim* (without delay). To my dismay, the supervisor declined to help. He admitted never placing a temporary pacemaker. Moreover, no one in the hospital at the time had the required skill to perform this life-saving task – and time was of the essence, with two lives at stake.

I dialled 999 – the UK national emergency number: 'I need an ambulance now. I need to go to a hospital now.'

The outside operator sounded perplexed: 'But you are in a hospital already. Why do you need another one?'

'I need an ambulance now, to take a patient to a specialist hospital. Where is the nearest heart hospital?'

I continued: 'Please hurry, the patient is pregnant. Her heart is beating too slowly. I cannot feel the baby moving.'

With the urgency understood, an ambulance arrived minutes later with orders to head for Hillingdon hospital, a noted cardiology centre.

'Take us to Hillingdon now – Yes, sirens and all lights flashing!'

I called my supervisor again. This time, I gave the orders: 'Please cover the hospital. Notify nearby Hillingdon hospital of our pending arrival. They must be ready to install a temporary pacemaker within minutes of our arrival.'

The patient needed attention in the ambulance. She continued to pass in and out of consciousness coincident with the intermittent decline in heart rate as we sped with lights flashing and sirens blaring. Within minutes of arriving at Hillingdon hospital casualty department the expert staff placed a temporary pacemaker and stabilized the patient.

'The baby is moving – alive.' A chorus of sighs of relief went round. The staff at Hillingdon hospital and back in Watford, including the supervisor, gave praise. I felt immense relief and made a personal note to honour this patient by completing a position in cardiology before embarking on my final career choice - a future hope.

The locum at Watford General ended at 9.00AM on the morning I walked into the Middlesex hospital for surgery. I did not return home. I took the train from Watford into London and the tube (subway) into central London. A passenger sitting opposite smiled: 'I see your suitcase. Off on a wee holiday?'

'Yes, you could say that.'

I alighted at Goodge Street tube station and walked into the main entrance of the Middlesex Hospital on Mortimer Street, carrying my 'holiday' suitcase.

Multiple tests and examinations filled the few days leading to surgery. The day of surgery remains a blur. Feelings of dread were mixed with relief at having arrived and being ready to take the plunge. The medical and nursing staff were all business, preparing me for the operation. They said little, likely assuming I, a physician, needed no explanations and, therefore, no words of comfort. At least they did not say 'you will be alright.' Those words would have rung hollow since I knew enough to know the long-term outcome remained uncertain. In return, I too switched into professional mode and feigned composure despite the turmoil of feelings inside. Was this the end? I took some comfort in silence knowing that I had taken out life insurance soon after I qualified. At least my mother and sister would benefit should I not survive.

I recall a sense of gratitude at waking up after the surgery, albeit disorientated, having headaches similar to those following the air encephalogram and being blurry eyed with double vision that lasted for days.

The nursing staff blindfolded me to reduce the visual problems. Mr Williams crept up to my bed unannounced. I recognised his voice: 'Your surgery was somewhat successful. We removed most of the growth.... we had to go in via your face (not inside the nose), but the scar should hide well since you wear spectacles.' I reached out my hand into a black space. A hand squeezed mine. Much needed comfort at last.

No one discussed the degree of success of the operation or my prognosis. In retrospect, the caring staff remained truthful in their silence. In 1978 many unknowns surrounded my condition and the outcomes following surgery. Medical and surgical advancements for prolactinoma were in their infancy. The relevant medical literature only begins to 'take off' after 1979. No one offered, or could offer, the answer to the question I wanted to hear: 'When (not if) can I resume my career?' Also, in the 1970s, a pervasive culture by medical personnel meant speaking indirectly about certain conditions with a serious diagnosis and prognosis. They used 'growth', 'lump' or other euphemistic term rather than 'cancer' or 'tumour'. As for prognosis, a 'let us wait and see' approach prevailed. Doctors avoided discussions of uncertainties and unknowns. Most patients, including me, preferred doctors to be straight when giving bad news.

Mr Williams offered mixed consolation when pressed: 'The tumour is benign.... but likely to grow again.'

I reacted as a typical patient. I only heard 'benign' the term I wanted to hear. My subconscious filed the remainder for later digestion. Guarded news may best be delivered in short 'sound-bytes' preferably repeated later when talking to a patient, healthcare professional or not.

The peculiar type of headache that I first experienced following the air encephalogram continued for weeks following surgery. Also, I developed an insatiable thirst due to diabetes insipidus, primarily due to an in-balance of hormones governed by the pituitary gland that control the conservation of water via the kidneys. What an irony! Actions of anti-diuretic hormone (ADH), a key hormone controlled by the pituitary gland, had been my main research project in New York during the summer internship in 1971. Back to being a patient, rather than a laboratory rat, urine came out as fast as I could replenish fluid by drinking several litres of water per day and through the night. This is no typical thirst to quench. I looked away from flower vases in the hospital as I craved water. This thirst remained unquenchable for weeks.

Maureen, my flat mate, moved out to allow mother to stay and care for me. Mother's employers in Buckinghamshire gave compassionate leave. This became a mixed blessing. She remained visibly devastated by my illness, uncertain prognosis and what the future may or may not hold for me as a doctor. In her eyes, I had earned my place in this hallowed discipline and now I was on the wrong side of the bed: 'All those years of study......'

I tried to hide my despair, but friends saw through the forced smiles.

One learns the value of true friendship when 'the chips are down'. Maureen continued to help with the rent. Others invited me to stay as I convalesced. The superintendent from Frimley Park, Captain Bignall, offered a place for convalescence. I declined with grateful thanks due to the need to stay close to the Middlesex hospital in central London. My treatment included high-dose corticosteroids and other medications essential to correct any deficiencies of a pituitary remnant.

I had the wish, but not the courage, to start searching for work. I joined the unemployed. The unemployment office required weekly visits to prove intent to find work before being given benefits. I smile at the memories of attempting to explain to the clerk behind a grill in a windowless office of my inability to work the preceding week. This demeaning exercise repeated over several weeks. A long queue snaked outside of the building. Typically, we waited outside more than one hour regardless of the weather. The policy for any unemployment benefits required the unemployed person to seek work at his/her prior level and trade.

People before me haggled with the window clerk over this requirement. The clerk needed convincing of my only work choice: 'Surely you can see that I cannot work as a doctor at the moment! I am on high-dose drugs.......No, I am not a drug addict.... I mean steroids, ...I have diabetes insipidus.... yes, I mean diabetes. No, I do not need insulin but my type of diabetes is serious, all the same. No, I do not know when I can return to medicine.... I might need radiotherapy.... I mean X-ray therapy to my head....... Yes, I promise to keep looking for work as a doctor.'

Jobs were advertised in the premier medical journals but vacancies for top-tier posts required contacting the individual consultants and in-person interviews. Junior doctors sought work around the British Isles. Rotations at SHO level typically lasted six months. This meant looking for the next post soon after starting a new position. Since qualifying as a doctor, I stayed within London and wanted to remain there, not the least to have access to medical specialists for my own healthcare.

At that time, I could not face any more disappointments. Instead, I filled days juggling the medications, having blood tests and attending remedial practical classes to improve the chance of passing the MRCP II practical. Explanations to known medical colleagues were unnecessary. Word spread. Most wished me 'all the best.' A few crossed the street to avoid any interaction rather than face having to commiserate. The medical community is tightly knit. Moreover, my face and demeanour told the whole story. Apart from the visible scar, facial swelling, and acne from high-dose corticosteroids, despair is difficult to hide from eyes trained to read physical signs.

Timing of the MRCP Part II practical examination coincided with readmission to hospital for follow-up because the prolactin levels remained elevated, albeit no longer 'sky-high'. This time the sun shone in my favour. By random allocation, the Royal Free Hospital School of Medicine, world famous for liver disease, hosted the MRCP II practicals. Back to 'liver' at last! I felt confident about passing that examination and returned happily to the Middlesex hospital after a 'good day's work'. I treated myself to a long overdue haircut, shampoo and set at a salon opposite the hospital. The stylist remarked at my cheerful demeanour despite the visible 'battle scar'. She congratulated me: 'Well done. You survived an unfortunate accident.' I did not correct her.

My future remained uncertain. Follow-up tests confirmed only a partially successful operation. I had to wait and see if permanent pituitary insufficiency developed with the lifelong requirement for several hormone supplements and medical supervision. The headaches lessened. The excessive thirst resolved but gynaecological symptoms continued and prolactin levels hovered above the normal range values. Nevertheless, after two months of recuperation and the MRCP II diploma under my belt, I felt physically and psychologically strong enough to try once more to step back onto the career ladder. So far, what remained of the pituitary continued to function adequately according to the litany of hormone tests.

My caring medical and surgical teams tried without success to dissuade me from returning 'into the lions' den' of hospital medicine: 'You are still at junior level…. the most physically demanding stage of an academic medical career.'

Word about my situation spread through London university to King's College and the professors associated with the intercalated BSc in Physiology. Dr Lewis, professor of statistics at Charing Cross Hospital and now working for the UK government, offered me a position in statistics in his office. But I set my heart on returning to medicine, preferably the academic and demanding kind.

Follow-up tests showed the pituitary remnant continued to function allowing me to successfully be weaned off corticosteroids and pituitary supplements. The caring medical and surgical team gave me permission to re-enter medical practice – with a provision:

'If you must go back (into medicine), at least try something like general practice – something less demanding that you can control in terms of hours.'

Well, I might as well give it a try. My response aimed to please the advisers rather than myself. The money would come in handy too as savings dwindled. I took a short-term locum in a solo general practice in London to substitute for a doctor who became seriously ill. This 'lock-up' practice specified hours for seeing patients. A remote agency on-call system covered after hours.

Well, this is a start and manageable.

The patients queued outside until the doors opened at 10.00AM. The office manager shut the doors promptly at 4.00PM. House calls, becoming unusual by 1978, were considered exceptional and only for the surrounding vicinity within walking distance. *I can do that.*

I embarked on a world away from the medical practice I knew and thrived on - bustling, demanding critical care within a busy, large teaching hospital. Thus far, most patients I had cared for were seriously ill and only too grateful for any intervention. Several first came into my care when unconscious, on life support – no conversations possible. In contrast, some patients in general practice requested medications I deemed unnecessary and inappropriate such as antibiotics for a viral infection, such as the common cold. They became dismayed at my response: 'No need, you have a viral infection that is not improved by antibiotics.' A mother considered her baby had 'the measle.' I had no colleague to consult for a second opinion as I scoured unsuccessfully looking for a bright red rash on the dark skin of a baby born to Jamaican parents.

An urgent call came to see a patient at home in the neighbourhood. She became acutely breathless on climbing stairs. The patient, a 35-year-old woman, sitting on the stairs and unable to ascend, showed obvious signs of acute heart failure. The giveaway 'strawberry' tongue is a textbook sign of scarlet fever with complicating heart problems (myocarditis). She needed admission to hospital without delay. I happily informed the patient that the ambulance team would take her to the best place nearby - my old hospital - Royal Brompton.

I recall well the final patient I examined in general practice. This young woman had persistent shoulder pain attributed by another practitioner to a rotator cuff injury. After physical examination, I remained unconvinced about the former diagnosis. She needed persuading to take time off work to go to a hospital for a radiograph of the shoulder and arm. Later I called the hospital to discover her diagnosis of metastatic cancer to the bone and liver from the breast. She needed hospital treatment and follow-up.

I had enough of general practice. More likely, general practice had enough of me. The pituitary function tests remained acceptable. I no longer needed supporting medications. Time had come, sink or swim, to attempt to re-enter hospital medicine where I could follow through with patients, especially the critically ill. My conviction to pursue gastroenterology remained. However, I needed to improve my knowledge of cardiology, a gap made obvious by the recent locum experience at Watford General. The chance of landing any post in the highly competitive field of cardiology would be slim at best, given my own medical history and desire to ultimately pursue a different speciality. Regardless, I had nothing to lose. Why not shoot for the top?

Chapter 12: Sword of Damocles

All these years hence, I marvel at gaining an interview at the prestigious London Chest Hospital (LCH) for a coveted post as Senior House Officer (SHO, similar to Senior Resident or Fellow in America) in cardiology. Despite the recent hurdle of passing the MRCP Part II examination (akin to Internal Medicine 'Boards' in the US) from a hospital bed, the odds were stacked against me. My job application made clear I had no intention of pursuing a career in cardiology. Moreover, I continued to recover from major surgery and faced possible radiotherapy. I could not hide the external battle wounds – a scar on a face still bloated and with acne from lingering side effects of high-dose corticosteroids. The medical profession knew about my health issues. In the 1970s patient-doctor confidentiality remained a gentlemen's (informal) agreement rather than based on any formal process as when HIPAA, the Health Insurance Portability and Accountability Act came into effect in the US in the 1990s.

When the caring medical team declared me medically fit to work, they warned: 'You are not out of the woods.' I knew I faced an uncertain future from within that forest. My health status circulated around the tight, well-trodden, halls of academic medicine. No doubt references from prior employers and my own healthcare team included salient details about the uncertain prognosis. Surgery had been only partially successful and tumour expansion likely would recur.

Several professionals advised against any further pursuit of a medical career, let alone a demanding speciality within academic medicine. Nevertheless, no one underestimated my determination to stay the course. However, all advised against pursuing gastroenterology and hepatology: 'Take up a less challenging profession.' This translated into 'We do not think you will have the physical stamina' and 'Don't waste your time and energy or ours on a futile pursuit.'

Worse, I set my mind on taking a detour via a SHO position in cardiology. This side-step seemed perfectly reasonable to me but irrational to many. I sought to fill a crucial gap in my ongoing medical education 'above the diaphragm.' In contrast, medical advisors emphasised the chance of gaining an interview as 'next to zero.' In addition to being handicapped by personal medical baggage, I sought to occupy a highly competitive post coveted by future cardiologists - a steppingstone to their illustrious careers in heart disease.

Hostility to me as an outsider, and especially one destined to quit medicine for health, if not anticipated family obligations, became obvious. Regardless of health, childless women of my age, considered 'getting on' at 28 years, surely soon would pause their medical careers to start a family. Interviewers and employers were not permitted to broach directly delicate subjects such as health or planning a family. Instead, they skirted the issue by asking for any reason to anticipate a shortfall in work commitment. Leaving medicine, however transitory, to start a family never crossed my mind. I was hanging on for dear life and taking one step at a time to salvage my only child - a hard-fought career. Hopefully, the interview panel would see my resolve – 'I will make it, you shall see.' (Chapter 1. 'So, you want to be a doctor?').

On the day of the interview, I took the tube (London Underground) and a bus to Bonner Road in Bethnal Green, East London, an underdeveloped, working-class suburb in 1978. The catchment area served many poor people and with a predominance of ethnic minorities. At that time, the LCH belonged to a circuit of elite speciality hospitals. As a training hospital in heart, as well as lung, diseases the experience and reputation were excellent especially given the ethnic and social diversity of patients. The LCH, founded in 1848, provided great need to care for patients with lung diseases, especially tuberculosis and industrial lung diseases, as well as heart diseases. The hospital closed in 2015 as cardiology speciality care became consolidated and transferred to nearby teaching hospitals, such as St. Bartholomew's.

The LCH was in its heyday in the summer of 1978 when I applied for a job to commence that autumn.

Several candidates already had assembled in the adjacent waiting room when I entered. I recognised no one, all aspiring cardiologists except me. The candidates chatted among themselves using first names and sharing anecdotes. They knew each other. A few gave knowing nods and side glances towards me indicating 'she is not one of us - an outsider.'

I noted silently with a practiced forced smile: 'Ah good, there are two other female candidates. That means the professors are willing to consider women at LCH.'

To my surprise, the usher called my name first, well ahead of the appointment time. Remaining candidates remained silent as all eyes followed me to the door leading to an inner room. The interview panel of several senior cardiologists and chest physicians assembled in the spacious, otherwise empty, 'T-shaped', room behind a long rectangular table. A picture of The Last Supper flashed across my mind as I walked down the long narrow stem of the 'T' to the single wooden chair facing the Who's Who in the hospital and cardiology circuit. The chairman in the centre nodded silently to recognise my entrance. In roll call style, the interviewers introduced themselves: 'I am Dr Bacon.... I am Dr Honey....'

A spontaneous smile to the panel, remembering I skipped breakfast.

From the left side of the panel: 'So, clearly, you want to be a cardiothoracic specialist since you worked for Professor Turner-Warwick at "Brompton" (the Professorial Unit in lung diseases)?'

'No. I want to be a gastroenterologist, actually, a hepatologist.'

Silence. Puzzled looks and raised eyebrows from left to right. Several panellists shuffled papers from within their folders.

From the right side of the panel: 'Hmm.... So, why pursue cardiology?'

'During weekend work as a locum doctor, I came across a pregnant woman in heart block. She needed a pacemaker urgently. No one at the hospital could perform such a procedure in time, including my supervisor, a gastroenterologist. I had to jump into an ambulance with this patient and head to the nearest heart hospital for emergency placement of a temporary pacemaker. Fortunately, the lady and baby did well. Still, I believe that every practicing doctor should know how to perform such life-saving procedures. When I become a hepatologist, I will come across patients with heart disease. I want to be able to care for the whole patient.'

Blank faces. More silence. More shuffling of papers.

I continued: 'I believe all organs are connected. A hepatologist should know what is going on above, as well as below, the diaphragm. While at "Brompton", I discovered two patients with all the hallmarks of sarcoidosis (a specific lung disease) and all the features of primary biliary cirrhosis (a designated liver disease recently coined primary biliary cholangitis)– once we looked further. Professor Turner-Warwick agrees I should write up these case reports for publication.'

The professors conferred among themselves but drew on their years of experience at the bedside to conceal any thoughts. Expressionless faces stared in my direction.

My mind raced: 'When will they get to the elephant in the room?' I hid the tell-tale purple markings over each temple denoting future radiotherapy by growing my hair strategically. However, with good vision and a smaller distance between candidate and interviewers, a panel would see the facial scar and signs of large-dose corticosteroids. Failing that, my medical history records were open before them.

A long silence. Heads nodded in unison. Here it comes. The chairman cleared his throat:

'We know about you, Dr Fagan.' No commiseration – all business. Several panel members closed their folders. They seemed in a hurry to move on to the first candidate.

'We understand you are cleared to practice medicine - for now. Can we assume you will not need time off during the six months position? As you must know, cardiology is a busy and demanding specialty, especially at our hospital ....'

My future remained uncertain given the unknown prognosis. I had to be truthful:

'I cannot guarantee anything regarding time off for more treatment; however, I promise I will let my supervisor know. Importantly, I will let everyone know if I feel unable to conduct my work at the highest level.'

I took this cue to voice my resolve: 'I wish you all to know.......,' but the chairman interrupted me: 'No need. Thank you.'

This interview seemed doomed. More blank stares and some mumblings among the interviewers, too far away to overhear.

I could not wait to get out of there.

Pause.

Chairman: 'Does anyone on the panel have another question for Dr Fagan?'

Silence except for the remaining closing of folders in unison and more nods; their minds made up.

'Since no one does, again, we thank you for coming here today.'

I mustered a feeble thank you, pushing back the chair with a loud scrape. I knew what my advisors would retort: 'We told you so.' I headed down the long narrow corridor towards the door, fighting back the tears. *Try not to race for the exit. Preserve your dignity.* I concluded the end to this inadequate interview signalled the finale to my medical career. No institution would take me on after this miserable performance. My vulnerability usurped resolve. Word would spread of the need for future treatment and uncertain prognosis. Radiotherapy and more surgery were the only options in 1978. Why did I hold any hope this interview would go well? From the panel's perspective, who would want to risk taking me on?

Junior doctors are the workhorses of the profession. Senior medical staff rely on them day-in, day-out (and nights too) and through thick and thin to cover the patients. Strong, healthy males have quit such positions – why take the risk of hiring a vulnerable person and female, to boot? These thoughts flashed by as I fumbled to find the doorknob, difficult to see as the tears became unstoppable. At least the panel only saw my back. One way to save face.

My mind was no longer in the room. I ignored murmurings coming from the panel, no doubt discussing my hopeless situation. I did not wish to hear any more. *Take deep breaths.* I tried to control the sobs joining tears.

Back to reality. The chairman called out: 'Oh, Dr Fagan, one more thing...'

I could not turn around. Too much pride for them to see me in such a state. They would not remember me anyway. I would never join their ranks as an outsider. More fumbling attempts to open the door. I did not wish to hear rejection. I wanted to run.

'We agree, unanimously, you have the (top) position with Drs Honey and Bacon. Do not tell the candidates in the waiting room. Please wait outside until all are done. Congratulations.'

I stopped, too stunned to reply and too embarrassed to turn around as the tears streamed relentlessly onto my blouse. Unlikely they heard another feeble 'thank you' as I choked back the sobs. Hopefully, a nod of ascent and a wave back to the panel from behind would suffice.

Into the waiting room after gently closing the door. The interviewees stared at me, red-faced, puffy-eyed, wet blouse, distressed. Their body language spoke volumes: 'Poor thing, whoever she is. Got a beating in there.' Some vocal commiserations: 'Better luck next time.' Several smiles followed my way as they must have thought: 'What did she expect for an outsider with no prior training in cardiology?'

Chapter 13: A turning point – just in time

The six-month SHO post in cardiology at the London Chest Hospital (LCH) flew by. The staff welcomed me on two fronts. They accepted me into their fold, this would-be outsider. Interventional cardiologists taught me many types of cardiac interventions, including how to implant a temporary pacemaker, in honour of the patient I encountered as a locum at Watford (Chapter 11. 'Physician, heal thyself'). Mrs Buxton, the lady who shared her home with me during clinical training years (1972-1975), once more welcomed 'her' student to stay. First impressions stick. The daily drive from South London over Tower Bridge to LCH provided time for reflection. I drove past landmarks including St. Paul's Cathedral, historical wharves, later to become Canary Wharf, and streets made famous by Charles Dickens. Plans to redevelop the East End of London, including The Docks, were repeatedly floated and shelved in my time. Few imagined this downtrodden, neglected area of London would host the Olympic Games in 2012.

Good news came when my own healthcare team postponed radiotherapy since the prolactin levels, although elevated, stabilised. Despite residual symptoms and a cautionary three-day stint in the Middlesex hospital for gastroenteritis, I completed the job with a pat on the back and a 'well done' from my superiors. This recognition and ability to stay the course bolstered my confidence to pursue becoming a gastroenterologist and hepatologist – but how, where and when? The lingering symptoms, albeit less than before surgery, served as a constant reminder of future uncertainties. No specific medication had been approved to shrink the residual tumour. The Sword of Damocles remained, albeit a smaller one for the moment. At least I identified the sword. Consequently, I hesitated to embark on a full training program in gastroenterology (GI) which typically lasted more than four years at that time.

In 1979, the Hammersmith hospital in west London advertised a suitable next-level position as a Registrar and Research Fellow in GI. As with LCH, this prized post offered endless potential in association with the unique Royal Postgraduate Medical School (RPMS). On paper, my credentials met the job requirements. Moreover, I worked for the same consultants (attendings) on the GI Unit in 1977, a year before the pituitary surgery. They seemed unaware of my health issues during that earlier time. I revealed to no one in my workplaces prior to 1978 any medical issues. My work record through to the day of surgery remained flawless. Over many years, I strategically engineered the timings of multiple attempts at diagnosis with endless tests and hospital stays to coincide with public holidays, nights and rare weekends earned off duty.

Now, the medical world knew me as a patient. I needed advice on pursuing such a demanding career preceded by lengthy training. I trusted the GI consultants at Hammersmith to give frank and unbiased advice on the odds of succeeding. Consequently, I waited until beyond the closing date of their advertised post to contact them. No doubt many suitable applicants with equally stellar credentials and without medical baggage applied. Out of respect, I wished to avoid putting the consultants in the awkward position of considering, and rejecting, my application. Back then, and hypothetically, an employee could not be refused a position on health grounds alone if deemed medically fit to practice; however, why take on someone with my health history when many candidates of excellent health competed for such a coveted post? I sought advice, not sympathy or pity, for this disadvantaged colleague knocked down but not out.

Memories poured in as I entered the Hammersmith hospital on Du Cane Road in West London. The hospital has an unimposing facade for such a hallowed institution. Familiar sounds of guard dogs barking brought me back to earth. The hospital shares a wall with Wormwood Scrubs prison. The junior doctors' on-call quarters faced the prison. No need for an alarm clock with the chorus of barks guaranteed before 6.00AM.

Three years had passed since I worked there. Six more sets of SHOs would have completed their rotations. Much top-grade water already passed under that venerated bridge.

My letter to Dr Chadwick, the senior consultant in gastroenterology, requested we meet informally – not an interview as such, at least not in my mind. His reputation as an outstanding academic gastroenterologist made him a popular choice for trainees. Equally important in my mind, Dr Chadwick dealt even-handedly and fairly with patients and staff alike. I trusted his judgement and recalled well how he counselled patients faced with life-threatening diagnoses and difficult decisions.

'I hope you remember me from back in 1977. I am only seeking advice.'

He smiled in recognition: 'Of course, I do. You look strong. How are you doing now?'

Dr Chadwick knew my medical history 'through colleagues.' He acknowledged the uncertain prognosis and nodded knowingly as I filled in the gaps: 'Do you believe you could do the job (as Registrar/Research Fellow)?'

I noted *the* job rather than *a* job and replied quickly to dismiss any inference of an offer: 'Yes, I do… but no, I am not here today for *the* job. I came to ask your advice about my prospects in gastroenterology.'

He did not respond immediately. Instead, he talked about his research interests in gut permeability. We shared these common interests and briefly discussed the merits and challenges in that field. My physiology BSc module in water and salt transport across membranes piqued his interest. We entered a mutual comfort zone discussing science. For a moment, I forgot my health situation and the purpose of my visit. We focused on how his research could be applied to new-born babies and the later development of allergies.

After a pause, Dr Chadwick asked: 'Can you start in three weeks?'

'Please, you must understand, I came here for advice about pursuing a career in GI, given the physical demands and lengthy training needed. I want to be a gastroenterologist; however, as you know, my future health is uncertain. I purposely timed our meeting until well after the closure of applications for your Registrar's post. I am not trying to apply for the position after the close. I know such a wonderful job is beyond reach given my medical situation.'

Calmly and without hesitation he repeated the question: 'Can you start in three weeks?'

Whatever reservations I felt due to an uncertain future, my heart and self-esteem soared with exhilaration knowing someone trusted my ability to do a good job, despite the odds. Dr Chadwick took a calculated risk employing me but decided the benefits were in our favour. He trusted me to put first the welfare of patients and reveal to him health challenges should I begin to falter. With that agreement, I accepted his job offer. No more was discussed about my health, then, or subsequently. True to form, he treated me equitably with others – no handicaps, no exemptions. In return, I no longer hid my health issues and shed those shackles worn silently for years - a liberating experience.

In the four years at the Hammersmith Hospital (1979-1983), I never missed a day off work, had papers published in peer-reviewed journals and began a doctoral research program (MD in the UK) on gut permeability. The GI department wished me to pursue a Master of Science degree (MSc) in biochemistry, a traditional path trod by Dr Chadwick and several researchers in his department. I preferred to study Immunology, a field blossoming with equally wide relevance in medical practice and research. Dr Chadwick graciously agreed.

Professor Keith Peters, head of the RPMS, signed off on the MSc application and provided funding through a grant from the postgraduate school to cover tuition fees: 'I expect you to bring back the gold,' - a euphemistic phrase for coming top of the class. And that I did, when awarded the only distinction in immunology in the 1982 class at Chelsea College (later merged with KCL).

My detour into cardiology and respiratory medicine paid dividends when I encountered patients on the GI wards with multiple medical issues above and below the diaphragm. Later, the practical skills learned at the London Chest Hospital served me well. I had the confidence and experience to pass catheters and lines into blood vessels within the chest to deliver fluids and monitor critically ill patients. Years later I applied this extra knowledge when working in biotechnology developing drugs for cardiac and lung diseases. Nothing learned in medicine goes to waste.

There is more to tell regarding the kindness and consideration of strangers. By 1979, I saved enough money as a deposit to secure a mortgage through a building society. In those days, a potential home buyer had to prove a track record of regular savings over several years. I set my heart on a two-bedroomed terraced house in West London and planned two weeks of holiday time to move in. I radiated excitement – a home, at last. A medical friend offered to share the down deposit and monthly payments. My friend backed out, citing financial difficulties, three days before closing on the house and after I agreed to relinquish my hospital room to another doctor. I raced to the accommodations' department within the medical school to ask permission to stay until I found an alternative roof over my head.

'No. Sorry. We cannot extend your stay. Your room is already allocated to a doctor arriving from abroad as soon as you move out.'

All those memories of being denied a roof over my head came back with a vengeance: 'I am on call these next two days and have no free time to go looking for a place to live.'

'Well, you are due a couple of week's holidays. Why don't you look at our bulletin board for nearby rental accommodation and then go home to your family for a few days' rest?'

At last, a turning point. I plucked up the courage and without shame continued: 'I need your help. I am almost 29 years old but have nowhere to go. I need a home of my own.'

The housing officer nodded in understanding as she looked at my forlorn face: 'Why don't you sit here with a nice cup of tea while I work on this for you? I won't be long.'

True to her word, her department worked with finance to provide an interest-free loan over ten years to cover the deposits and other costs to complete the closing. Two days later I moved into the terraced house, my first home. The previous owner, an elderly man, disabled and recently widowed, left all furniture and household items. I walked in and put on the kettle for tea, also provided.

Another turning point came during the first few months at the Hammersmith with approval of bromocriptine for my medical condition. Over the years as a doctor, I came across patients who declared certain medicines as miracles when their lives turned around - and the same happened to me. Within two months of starting oral therapy, my residual symptoms subsided and prolactin levels normalised. For the first time in decades, I felt well. On reflection, I had been ailing, feeling sub-par, for more than half of my life. Better still, I escaped radiotherapy. Bromocriptine became my mainstay for 22 years until I stopped treatment reluctantly after a neurosurgeon in the USA convinced me a recurrence after so long would be unlikely. By discontinuing bromocriptine after more than two decades, I said goodbye to a long-standing friend. Finally, I closed that door, that chapter. From a health perspective, I never looked back.

Several lessons from this Chapter stand out; keep looking forward and follow what excites you. Challenge boundaries and do not be afraid of rejection. Find the courage within to ask for help. Do not be ashamed of circumstances beyond your control. Knowledge does not go to waste.

Chapter 14: A patient who changed my life

Extract adapted from the British Medical Journal 1993; 307: 1330 with permission:

*O*L *was 13 years old. I knew him less than one week. Five years later I moved and changed the direction of my career as a consequence of our brief encounter.*

He became ill in the summer of 1985. The 'flu-like illness progressed relentlessly to acute liver failure. Sporadic non-A, non-B (non-C hepatitis) is the most common, presumed viral cause of acute liver failure in Britain and United States. The agent/s remain unidentified and survival without liver transplantation remained below 20% at that time.

We met when he was in grade four hepatic encephalopathy – deeply unconscious, on life-support. His only chance of survival was with a new liver. Two days after liver transplantation he sat in a chair and tuned into his radio.

One week later the liver failure recurred. The clinical picture resembled a haemorrhagic fever. He bled from multiple sites and died soon after. The liver graft was swollen and haemorrhagic. There was little evidence of rejection. The surgical anastomoses were faultless.

Electron microscopy showed virus-like particles resembling arboviruses in his original (native) liver. By early 1988 we had collected two further cases of recurrent liver failure within a week of first liver transplantation for acute liver failure of unknown cause. Importantly, abundant virus-like particles were detected by electron microscopy in the liver grafts if the liver failure recurred. There was sufficient evidence to implicate a novel virus agent. We needed a scientist to clone its genome.

A turning point came in October 1988 that altered my career path. The designated (-80°C) refrigerator complete with safety alarms and containing the liver bank of research specimens thawed mysteriously while I was on a world lecture tour advocating for hepatitis B virus vaccines. Undeterred, I restarted the liver bank collection, this time determined to tackle the molecular biology hunt myself. By 1990, we had collected nine more cases with paired liver samples before and after liver transplantation.

In 1991, I moved from King's College Hospital to the Royal Free Hospital School of Medicine to enter the world of molecular virology and cloning, aided by a full-time senior research fellowship from the Wellcome Trust and a grant from the Digestive Diseases Foundation. First, before I could embark on finding a novel virus, I needed to exclude the usual virus suspects and their variants as covert causes of acute liver failure. Only after an exhaustive negative search, could I switch to positively hunting down a new culprit. The road ahead would be long and winding.

Full time research can be lonely. Fifteen years of clinical practice made me dependent on the daily rewards that come inevitably from dealing with patients. Laboratory science can be an empty experience - with nothing to show for weeks of labour. I had to justify repeatedly to other clinicians why I relinquished a unique and secure post with a promising career trajectory as a senior clinician in the largest Liver Unit in the world in pursuit of science to solve an uncommon disease.

Once more, I earned the reputation as an outsider. In 1989, my 'obscure' research interests contrasted with the world of liver disease focused on the newly discovered hepatitis C virus (HCV). A test (anti-hepatitis C antibodies) to detect this infection revealed thousands of infected patients in the UK and worldwide. In contrast, the UK reported less than 50 cases per year of acute liver failure of unknown cause and only a handful recurred after liver transplantation. I justified my odd pursuit based on a long-held belief that uncommon cases in medicine and science are fertile grounds for learning about the more common diseases – treasure your exceptions. As proof, I pursued the unusual as a main theme for my doctoral (MD 1989) thesis on the unsuspected detection of hepatitis B virus.

I became a student again, this time at the hands of molecular virologists half my age who shared the intricacies of their craft. Financially, I depended on annual renewals of a research grant from the Wellcome Trust. For the ensuing five years (1991-1995), every December I wondered if I would be able to pay my mortgage the following year. My move from South to North London after eight years at KCH required lifestyle changes. Back to the simple life. Down-sizing meant renting out my four-bedroom house in South London, buying a tiny flat within walking distance of the School of Medicine, taking in a flat-mate to share costs and selling my car. I walked to the laboratory several times daily and often at night and weekends as experiments incubated.

Working in closed containment facilities necessary when handling infectious agents is an isolating experience. A distant radio, tuned in to events of the first Gulf war in 1991, became my companion. However, science can be exhilarating especially after a long and delayed gestation. Buoyed by early mastery of basic techniques, I experienced a newly found joy when an experiment worked. The encouragement and camaraderie from young scientists in the same laboratory uplifted me.

Over time, I became one of them. As medical doctors passed through the laboratory to gain some research experience, the molecular biologists voiced their complaints to me: 'Those medics are not genuinely interested in research.'

With a friendly nod in my direction, these full-time career scientists added: 'They are not like us scientists. Their goal is for a quick publication to enhance their clinical careers.'

Progress on the project to discover a new virus (candidate hepatitis F) continued methodically, often laboriously, but positively. I spent two years excluding the usual virus culprits and their variant forms.

In 1993, after two years as a full-time laboratory scientist, I took the plunge and switched from excluding, to positively identifying, novel virus candidates. On DNA extracted from frozen liver samples, I used molecular probes designed specifically to detect conserved genetic sequences of viruses known to cause haemorrhagic disease.

These crucial experiments were expected to take months, if not years. Screening millions of clones containing possible and diverse genetic sequences is a needle-in-a-haystack approach. I soldiered on for a year. The early experiments to establish the validity of the technique worked. *I can do this!*

A trip to Tokyo in May 1993 to a triennial conference on viral hepatitis provided light relief from laboratory routines. Sharing scientific ideas with like-minded colleagues is sustenance for any researcher whose life revolves around test tubes, pipettes and centrifuges. More so for me in contrast with my former life, I missed the numerous daily interactions within a busy hospital setting.

As a virologist of renown, the Dean of the Royal Free Hospital School of Medicine, not surprisingly, took especial interest in the project. He appointed as my supervisor his 'right-hand man,' a molecular virologist of years' standing. During the conference in Tokyo the Dean introduced me to academic and business colleagues including a US-based pharmaceutical company with a virology focus. Their senior vice-president and senior virologist showed interest in investing in the project and invited me to their headquarters near Chicago. I returned from a short visit to Chicago excited about the prospect of additional funding. Support and assistance to enlarge the project would mean no longer being a one-'man' band at the bench.

My supervisor worked closely with the Dean for years and included his name on some scientific papers. He provided the Dean with updates on my return from America – great timing, I thought. A 'congratulations' posted by my supervisor on the incubator door indicated the growing clones inside were ready to be harvested and screened – a breakthrough!

He made an appointment for me to see the Dean - my time to shine, so I thought. I took pride in how far I had come with the project working single-handedly. I planned to emphasise my ongoing commitment and resolve, having completed the preparatory work. In my mind, I had proven capable of the task, so far. Soon I intended to submit molecular virology results for publication and to my sponsors (Wellcome Trust) to request additional funding for an assistant - more hands to the deck.

With a smile, clutching my laboratory notebook, I entered the Dean's office. As head of the School of Medicine, he projected a formidable figure. However, I did not feel intimidated. We knew each other more than ten years and shared a long-held interest in viral hepatitis, especially hepatitis B vaccination. I rehearsed the list of requests in my head: 'Thank you for seeing me – great timing – I have succeeded in... Now I need more funding......' More smiles:

'Good morning, Professor. Thank you for seeing me – great ....'

He interrupted my flow: 'We have transferred your project to that pharmaceutical Company near Chicago. Of course, you are welcome to stay on here if you can raise a grant to support yourself for different research; however, you must start over. Your current supervisor may be able to find some temporary laboratory space but, as you know, lab space is tight. The school has no spare money for clinical projects to help patients let alone academic research. You may have some access to the project in America but that remains undecided.'

Confused, I stammered out: 'But... but.... I don't understand. This is my project. I have built it up over 11 years and am at a critical....'

Pleas were ignored. He waved me out of the room. An office staff member pointed to the exit, as if I needed reminding.

My supervisor deflected any questions and protests: 'Well, that is up to the Dean.'

I had no choice but to continue working to prevent the delicate clones, months of work, going to waste. Like a ripe crop, they needed harvesting before the storm.

Abruptly, my supervisor stopped communicating with me as did the Dean's office. The administrative officers in the School of Medicine made clear they would not interfere with 'the Dean's business.'

The Dean refused to see me. My supervisor washed his hands of any interactions when I cornered him with obvious questions: 'How am I supposed to raise research money given my entire focus for three plus years on this project?'

Later, the School of Medicine's office staff indicated the Dean located a university hospital in Chicago 'willing to take you [me].' Any access to research facilities would be up to me. If I accepted this option, the RFHSM would pay me to work there for three years as a Senior Research Fellow, funded through the pharmaceutical company, except without research facilities and funding – a researcher *sine* research!

Without immediate access to research, the road ahead in the UK would be long if I pursued my career as a physician-scientist. Although I continued to publish papers within the broader scope of my known field, acute and chronic viral hepatitis, these would be insufficient to raise substantive grant monies to start over again. As a physician-scientist I needed to generate a new research project and publish findings before attempting to raise funding.

In addition, the Dean's proposal for the US benchmarked my salary on a UK-based scale for a senior research fellow, well below that of a senior physician in the UK let alone in the USA. The School and Dean ignored the significantly higher salary grade as a Lecturer at King's College Hospital - relinquished four years before to pursue this work. The officials declined to address these discrepancies in salary scale.

The Dean's office informed me in no uncertain terms that the research samples and liver collection must be ready for transfer to the American pharmaceutical company. Any hopes of having continuing access to the project depended on this cooperation.

The pharmaceutical company arranged collection via my supervisor and Dean without my knowledge. Company personnel from America swooped in on a private 'plane with their own US customs agent. Together, with little advance notice, we packed the samples in kilograms of dry ice. I handed over the laboratory samples and documents, including the precious collection of liver transplant material collected over more than a decade. The senior vice president of the company flew in separately from Asia to oversee the transfer. Clearly, this project represented a significant investment for the pharmaceutical company and School of Medicine.

I had medical contacts in America and made preliminary enquiries about transferring to a separate university in Chicago with hepatology colleagues who shared similar research interests in liver failure. I envisaged being near my beloved project in a university of my own choosing and one likely to provide immediate financial support and facilities for research – a much faster route to starting over again.

The Dean's office responded: 'You will go to the institution we have chosen, not one of your choosing. Otherwise, you will lose the generous salary negotiated by the Dean. You should be grateful the Dean has negotiated a three-year salary for you.'

'What about research money to start over again?'

'None is allocated. You will have to find that on your own.'

'What about access to my project?'

'That is up to the pharmaceutical company. You will have to negotiate with them once over in Chicago. Here is a letter of Agreement.'

'But the letter does not outline what access I will have to my project …'

'You need to transfer over to the medical Institution we have designated…'

'What about an American work permit (visa)?'

'That is up to you.'

Without access to research funds and laboratory space at the RFHSM and with immediate termination of the Wellcome research grant, I saw transferring to the USA as my only option.

Friends urged me to walk away – be done with all. I look back at my naïveté, holding out hope I would be treated equitably. Ironically, I never expected or wished to complete the project alone. All along, I aimed to develop and pass on to experts the project once beyond certain milestones. I see myself as a physician-scientist, with 'physician' coming first.

Screening for a novel virus is a marathon task best undertaken by a team of academic athletes with decades of experience in the field. Consider a great marathon on display to the world when a team of world-class scientists at Chiron Corporation, through ingenious molecular techniques, discovered hepatitis C virus in 1989.

The courage to walk away at the right time, from a business deal or otherwise, is a skill I learned the hard way. Some allies questioned me: 'Why did you pack up the samples and specimens collected over years and hand them over so willingly?'

By then, I knew I had lost the project. A university employee in the UK has few rights to her research and discoveries: 'Better to let the project go to skilled hands than be "killed" for lack of support.' Above all, I hoped some good would come out to benefit patients with recurrent liver failure.

Driven by heart, not head, I accepted to go out to the USA on their terms to the designated institution on the meagre UK-based research salary. The project had become my child. As a fretful mother concerned for the wellbeing of her creation, I continued to believe I would have some control over the project. I could not let go, at least not yet.

Chapter 15: Winning the battle, losing the war

Soldiers on the front line of battle rely primarily on their buddies for survival. For many, the more elevated view of fighting for king and country takes second place. In the past, I discovered the meaning of true friendship when faced with tough times. During 1993 – 1996 while attempting to salvage access to my research project (Chapter 14. 'A patient who changed my life.'), I learned that friends are not always those predicted to be there in times of need. Some in the Royal Free Hospital School of Medicine (RFHSM), and once supportive of my work, crossed the street when I passed nearby. The School of Medicine officials branded me a troublemaker and 'ungrateful for the generous deal' made on my behalf by the Dean.

Few took time to learn the truth behind that deal. Over five years I came fully funded and added prestige to the School. Another physician-scientist pursued a PhD on a different liver virus - hepatitis E virus – based on liver samples I collected over years. In return, at age 43 years, I found myself without income and research funds while filing for an American visa on my own volition, all without assistance from the RFHSM.

I rented out my flat and moved in with friends in rotation to minimise outstaying my welcome. These true friends themselves experienced challenging times. A highly educated medical couple from Bagdad, now living nearby, fled to London during the first Gulf War in 1991. They adopted me as family, sharing their home and food. They lost their former home and well-established, hard-earned livelihood in Iraq. Family members scattered across the globe. Their teenage children experienced disruptions in education but stoically studied the harder to catch up. I could relate to their resolve (Chapter 1. 'So you want to be a doctor?'). Every member, now a refugee, started over again. Another friend, a single parent with a baby and working from home to make ends meet, made room in her house, fed and welcomed me. None asked for payback.

My troubles paled into insignificance by comparison. Their struggles provide a fresh perspective. Despite facing setbacks, I retained many advantages to pick up the pieces of my life. Any frustration and distress reflected the lack of control over my career. While I faced making the best of a poor deal, these dear friends faced few choices and no deals. No obvious lights shone at the end of their tunnels. All took work at levels 'below their station' but seemed grateful for their lot. I seethed at mine. A glass half full versus half empty depends on one's prism of the world. My glass shattered.

The fate of our mother, now in her 70s and with failing eyesight due to aggressive glaucoma, required consideration. Mother, now retired, lived in Chelsea in a flat subsidised by the local council. I visited her briefly and infrequently due to workload, travel and other work-related distractions. She struggled to adapt to the fast pace of London made worse by failing vision. My sister, Mary, and I could not envisage her surviving in Chicago, known for brutally cold and protracted winters. I would be too busy to give sufficient care and attention. We saw her only option to emigrate to New Zealand. Mary, recently widowed and raising two teenagers, worked as a community-based nurse in a small town in the North Island. Mother, now resigned to her fate, agreed to relocate halfway across the world. The light in her eyes continued to dim in more ways than one.

While awaiting details of a US work permit, a research colleague in Glasgow, Scotland offered free laboratory space and access to chemicals and equipment to kick-start research again. I rented a room in a nearby students' residence and eventually spent two summers developing a project on hepatitis B, a familiar research field in which I had an established pedigree. Once more, the camaraderie of young molecular biologists buoyed my spirits and encouraged me to keep calm and carry on.

The RFHSM forbade any work within the same field as my beloved project. Worse, I became a pariah in the eyes of the UK medical community. Word spread of my ingratitude to the Dean and RFHSM. To gauge the chance of starting over in the UK, I applied for two positions as a consultant clinician; one aligned with a university in the west of England and another in a hospital on the outskirts of London. Rejection came quickly without recourse. Feedback filtered through a backchannel noted: 'She is overqualified.'

A typical work visa for the USA requires a sponsor and direct offer of work. Since the School of Medicine refused to be sponsor, I went 'whole hog' and applied under a limited independent visa category (E11). Enticingly, this category for exceptional persons comes automatically with a green card – denoting a 'resident alien.' An E11 holder and resident alien has validity to work in America beyond the two-year limit of a traditional work visa such as the H-1. An E11 visa with green card automatically opens a fast-track pathway to citizenship, not that I considered becoming an American citizen in 1993-1994. Fortunately, prior to and during my employment at the RFHSM, the media including television and newspapers (The Times: 12 August 1991: Mystery virus suspected of causing fatal liver disease), covered my work. My curriculum vitae supported an E11 visa category. No contest.

As an E11 visa holder, I keep company with John Lennon, Yoko Ono, some Olympians, and other persons of noted achievement. Resigned now to the 'generous' RFHSM offer to work in America, I booked a flight to Chicago in November 1994 to coincide with a large medical conference in liver disease. Once there, I rented a small apartment with access to the allocated hospital, Rush Presbyterian, St. Luke's Medical Center ('Rush'). Dr Jensen, a professor at Rush and an acknowledged hepatologist, had completed advanced training on the Liver Unit at King's College Hospital. Without hesitation, he offered me a clinical position in his department. Research opportunities would come later. My gratitude remains at being recognised as a human being with skills to offer.

My arrival at Rush in Chicago coincided with Thanksgiving, a national holiday across America, to honour pilgrims who celebrated their harvest after arriving on those shores in 1621. An administrator in the hospital invited me home. This is an important celebration in America when friends and family gather. A tradition is to take in a stranger to share this occasion. To this day, Thanksgiving remains my favourite public holiday in America.

Meanwhile, the quest to access the research on candidate hepatitis F continued back in the UK. The British Medical Association (BMA) agreed to take up my case against the RFHSM. Meanwhile, the Dean hired a personal lawyer. I learned only months later that the BMA had turned down the Dean's request for legal representation. The ensuing 18 months were consumed returning to the UK on several occasions, and at my expense, to build our case.

More obstacles followed. The medical licensing authorities in the State of Illinois required I pass further medical examinations to qualify to practice unsupervised in their State, regardless of recognition by Rush as a senior staff and faculty member.

A low point came in December 1995. I returned to the UK to prepare my case against the School of Medicine with assistance from the BMA. I planned to return to Chicago for Christmas. However, the day before, I slipped on ice outside the RFHSM and fractured my right forearm (radius and ulna). This accident required a hospital stay over Christmas following surgery with external pins and plates. Again, my dear friends from Iraq came to the rescue, housing and caring for me. I required assistance with tasks of daily living; washing hair, buttoning a shirt and any function requiring two hands. The next blow came when BMA counsel advised under conditions of employment for a university employee, I faced an internal tribunal at the RFHSM before taking my case through to a traditional (external) court. Worse, the tribunal panel would be selected by the head of the RFHSM - the Dean - the very person who excluded me from the deal he negotiated with the US pharmaceutical company. To ostensibly show fairness, an internal tribunal panel within the RFHSM included one or more members from outside the institution. However, timing of the tribunal coincided with input from the Dean on pending promotions of some panel members, including those outside the School.

I faced insurmountable odds. I remained in London for follow-up after surgery and physiotherapy to my arm and hand. Months later and after two days of tribunal hearings, the BMA upheld their original decision - I had been 'wronged.' Regardless, the internal tribunal staffed by the Dean, not surprisingly, voted against us. The tribunal panel gave two concessions. The RFHSM should have offered counselling on career choices and laboratory bench-space, albeit without funding for new research.

Subsequently, the RFHSM provided a 'counsellor', Robert Pointer, head of the gastroenterology department and well-known to the Dean. His role, on paper, was to listen to my side of the story, albeit after closure of the tribunal, and to give career guidance as recommended by the tribunal. Any salary from the RFHSM funded by the US Pharmaceutical Company, depended on meetings with this counsellor and accepting the clinical position in Chicago on a UK-based salary as a senior research fellow except without research funding, no laboratory space allocated and no access to an established research project.

Professor Pointer and I met a few times per recommendations of the tribunal. From the outset he made clear the RFHSM closed the chapter on my beloved research project. He refused to review my laboratory notebooks detailing the progress and disputing timelines raised during the tribunal. As to future bench space recommended by the panel, he offered none, justified by lack of corresponding research funding. He offered no career guidance except 'that is up to you.' My letters and communications to him as official intermediary for the School went unanswered. Months later when in Chicago, a hepatology colleague from the RFHSM contacted me independently with a personal offer of temporary bench space in his laboratory. Without research expenses and salary to remain in the UK, this offer remained moot.

Outside legal counsel, including two barristers who learned about my situation through friends, and the BMA advised me to move forward – close the door. Personal savings dwindled. Legal fees, if I hired a lawyer, would pile up over months, or more likely, stretch over years. Some allies likened my situation to a parish priest fighting the pope. This is no David-and-Goliath story. By early 1996, I was half-way through the three-year stipend provided by the pharmaceutical company and channelled through the RFHSM and with little to show towards restarting a research career. Understandably, research facilities in most academic institutions are offered to those with supporting grants as I duly obtained over prior successive years. A grant is needed to carry out high-level research and research data are needed to obtain a grant and feed that endless cycle. I found myself between the devil and deep-blue sea - in American parlance; 'between a rock and a hard place.' The mantra 'publish or perish' is one that most academics live by. The academic medical community is tightly interwoven. The chances of redeeming a research career in the UK for the foreseeable future would be slim.

In mid 1996, after 18 months of challenging the RFHSM I agreed with counsel and friends the time had come to close the door on this unhappy chapter. What prompted the change of heart, and mind, after so long? What prompted me to let go? I could move on because, by then, I built and invested in an alternative future path, now in America. No longer were all the eggs in one basket when I invested soul, spirit and limb in one solitary endeavour – the research project that consumed my life for years.

Resolute, I flew into London from Chicago and travelled directly to BMA house to resign from the RFHSM. Counsel advised me not to venture in person to the School. The Dean's office forewarned the BMA of signs posted on its front door denying my entry as a *persona non grata*. After the Dean's office accepted the resignation papers couriered from the BMA, I returned to Heathrow airport and caught a same-day flight to Chicago – this time on a one-way ticket.

By then, I learned the hard way how life's journey can involve starting over several times including in science and medicine. Universities in the UK typically own the rights to research generated by an employee. However, in my time, an unwritten understanding held the university employee who generated research of value would be 'recognised' - treated fairly. From then, I insist and advise others on all agreements being in writing and reviewed in depth to avoid any misunderstandings.

In America, US-based agreements between a research employee and university (employer) typically offer some recognition of ownership rights for the researcher. I know I am not alone in being side-lined. Over the years, several researchers in the UK reached out with comparable stories of being overlooked, ignored or side-lined by overriding university authorities. Transparency of rights of researchers on their discoveries with more equitable recognition of their contributions and sacrifices should encourage more to pursue research.

What happened to the project? I am not aware of any publications outside of mine relating to candidate hepatitis F. During the years 1994-1995 scientists and many virologists focused on hepatitis C and hepatitis C-like viruses and their potential impact within and without hepatology. Word filtered over months the pharmaceutical company shelved the project soon after transfer from the RFHSM. In June 1995, the pharmaceutical company published its discovery of a virus – GBV-C, then considered closely related to hepatitis C virus. Data published subsequently indicate only a minor role for GBV-C in liver and other diseases.

I never learned the full monetary value of the deal made in 1994 between the Dean of the RFHSM and pharmaceutical company in Chicago. Funds within the RFHSM for new projects, buildings and other developments remained limited during my time working in the School (1991-1994). The School cited repeatedly a lack of spare funds to expand my project or support me. My hope is this windfall went towards patient care. In 1995, the RFHSM opened a travel clinic headed by the Dean's daughter.

A decade would pass before the paths of Robert Pointer, the assigned 'counsellor', and mine would cross once more and under different circumstances (Chapter 17. 'Didn't we do well?!').

Chapter 16: Starting over, full circle

In mid 1996, with some relief and good timing, I accepted a secure and prestigious position at Rush Presbyterian St. Luke's Medical Center in Chicago (Rush) as a senior attending (consultant) and professor of internal medicine adding later also, of pediatrics. I joined the Hepatology Department headed by Dr Jensen, an esteemed American colleague I knew for some years. He recognised my training having spent time himself on King's Liver Unit and acknowledged the quirks of us Brits, even our dry sense of humour. A good start. Rush, named after Benjamin Rush, a signer of the Declaration of Independence, is a major institution in Chicago. Of equal importance to me, Rush makes an exception to accept and care for financially disadvantaged and marginalised patients who require emergent (urgent) care. *I can work here.*

Unfortunately, as an academic clinician-scientist, I started at Rush with a major disadvantage – no research grant. Moreover, all my recent publications focused on acute liver failure and candidate hepatitis F, considered an obscure topic by many. Without recent research accomplishments in hepatitis C, the 'flavour of the month', research funding remained hard to find. Grants are awarded on merit; however, as in business, topical issues attract funding and sponsorship. Research funding is a chicken and egg scenario – one needs to show accomplishment to obtain a grant. One needs money to fund that achievement. Obtaining laboratory space and facilities remain a challenge for many researchers. Not surprisingly, these too depend on grant funding – more chicken and plenty of egg. Despite these disadvantages, colleagues at Rush supported my appointment.

Beyond the privileges enjoyed as a senior member of a university faculty, I joined immigrants who seek success and personal freedom in the 'land of opportunity.' The processing of documents at two separate immigration centres in Chicago serves as a reminder of hurdles others less fortunate need to clear to obtain a foot in the door. On entry to the US (14th of November 1994), the Chicago O'Hare airport immigration authorities treated me with respect as a holder of an E11 visa. I waited alone in a comfortable room, akin to an upscale airport club lounge replete with refreshments. The authorities promptly printed out the coveted green card (which is pink!) with my solitary fingerprint and handed this with a smile and 'Welcome home!'

Subsequently, in December 1994, a letter from immigration requested I report back, this time to downtown, to repeat the solitary fingerprint; the first being considered substandard. I assumed this visit, as before, would be brief and cordial. Accordingly, I dressed business-style for work, briefcase in hand. By now, I outfitted myself with a padded coat, thick woollen hat, scarf, padded gloves and knee-high boots to brave the weather. Already at 07.00AM, an hour before opening time, a queue snaked around the office block. Many immigrants dressed inadequately for the Chicago winter. Few wore coats despite temperatures hovering below freezing point. None wore gloves or a hat. Their many languages reflected our diverse roots. Most sought work permits or came to defend their right to remain in America. I waved my E11 visa and green card at the immigration official surveying the growing line. Unceremoniously, the guard indicated I re-join the queue: 'Lady, no exceptions.' When the doors opened, now chilled to the bone despite several layers of clothing, I struggled to hold a pen to sign the entry log. The commanding officer for triage barked orders in English and Spanish. I understood little. Armed guards hovered.

After one hour, my turn came to hand in the documents. By then, thawed out sufficiently, I pushed the papers through a small window. A faceless voice spoke through the intercom: 'What are you doing down here? You're an E11. You need to go upstairs. Show this ticket to the guard on the stairs. Have a nice day.'

This is a story of 'upstairs-downstairs'. As with O'Hare airport, the immigration staff upstairs showed me into a comfortable room and offered refreshments. The officer handling my papers apologised for the delay. Hot tea and one thawed fingerprint later, I returned downstairs. Any frustration at this experience dissolved as I entered the main foyer. Some immigrants ahead of me in the outside queue continued to wait their turn. The line stretched further than before. The thermometer never reached above freezing that day.

My attention turned to work. Despite accomplishments and expertise, I required a license (American spelling) to practice medicine in the State of Illinois. By 1996, I notched more than 20 years as a qualified doctor including 15 as an academic gastroenterologist and hepatologist working in internationally recognised centres of excellence. My GI and hepatology training (Registrar level and below) encompassed 11 years compared with the more typical five years speciality training in the UK and three to four years for an American Fellow. I do not include the 15 months of extra training in lung and heart diseases. Moreover, I hold double qualifications to practice gastroenterology and hepatology. In the US, a physician may train in hepatology with little direct gastroenterology experience. Sub-speciality certification in transplant hepatology requires only one additional year of training. In contrast, I practiced as a transplant hepatologist for eight years at King's in the largest liver unit in Europe. My extensive training in hepatology preceded recognised certification in that speciality. I trained as SHO up to Lecturer level (equivalent to Assistant or Associate Professor in the USA), when certification bodies considered gastroenterology encompassed hepatology.

Regardless, I remained confident in applying for accreditation and a medical license in Illinois based on supporting credentials. I shared with celebrities the E11 visa status that denotes exceptional persons and comes automatically with a green card for establishing permanent residence in the USA. The E11 visa holds significance as a category awarded independently of any offer of employment. Moreover, I held the bonus of an invitation to join faculty in a large academic hospital and university in Chicago.

I arrived from Scotland to the Illinois Department of Professional Regulation (IDPR) situated in the Thompson Center in downtown Chicago. I looked forward to obtaining my license and assumed this would be a mere formality given my credentials. Not so.

Instead, I faced a hearing – court-room style without a jury – with a panel of 'judges'; non-descript and nameless persons.

A group of us 'defendants' sat in 'the dock'. One by one the panel called us forward. All defendants witnessed the deliberations. The defendant before me, a surgeon trained in South Africa, spent four years working at Cook County Hospital, situated adjacent to Rush. Unlike Rush, Cook County is a state-run institution for many patients from poor communities. Some patients are indigent and undocumented. Many have significant health issues. Surgeons working at Cook County Hospital have extraordinary experience in all aspects of healthcare including trauma and emergency surgery. Al Capone sent his victims there.

The surgeon from South Africa cut a fine figure. Well-dressed and mature, he projected dignity without arrogance. A panel member read out his resumé and appeal to grant a full license to practice rather than continuing his provisional one requiring supervision.

The panel promptly dismissed his appeal: 'We believe you (the surgeon) are trying to jump the queue and get into surgical practice in the US via the back door – denied.'

The surgeon, understandably aggrieved, spoke up: 'My supervisors are less experienced than I am. I have been a practicing surgeon for more than ten years and am widely trained in South....'

The panel promptly dismissed this surgeon mid-sentence. An usher showed him the door. My mind flashed back to the Dean in London dismissing me without cause.

'The next case is Dr Fagan, a microbiologist. She has worked in microbiology and pathology in England and is requesting a '036' (full) medical/surgical license to practice here in Illinois...'

Clearly misrepresented, I piped up: 'I am a hepatologist and gastroenterologist, graduated 20 years ago...'

'You may not address the Licensing Board unless invited. We have decided you will need to sit a remedial examination. You may go.'

As with the surgeon, I stood up and faced the panel: 'With what portion of my CV do you not agree? – I am fully trained in internal medicine, GI and hepatology and, yes, I spent four years in a molecular virology lab in London, England, but am fully trained to practice – and have been accepted at Rush Presbyterian....'

'As we said, you will need to sit the SPEX examination first before we grant a license. The administrator outside will give you details. Dismissed. The next case is.......'

The usher showed me the door.

The administrator in reception came straight to the point: 'You will need to take the SPEX examination.'

'What on earth is that?'

'I do not have details. The IDPR (Illinois Department of Professional Regulation) will send these to you. We at the IDPR recommend you drop by again in two- or three-weeks' time to submit more paperwork.

'But I have come all the way from Glasgow!' I added 'in Scotland.....in England' after seeing successive puzzled expressions.

'You will be notified when you need to come to Chicago to take the test.'

The administrator intimated that I should be grateful the IDPR exempted me from Board Speciality examinations in gastroenterology since I held certification by the Education Commission for Foreign Medical Graduates (ECFMG).

'I have five degrees, two with distinctions and the equivalent of your "Boards" (MRCP) and speciality recognition in internal medicine, gastroenterology and hepatology. Americans come over to King's Liver Unit to train, for goodness sakes.'

She seemed unconvinced, so I continued: 'I was invited to America and hold a distinguished E11 visa with automatic green card. What more do you people want to prove my capabilities?'

She softened her tone, seeing me upset: 'Well, the news is not all bad. At least you took and passed the English portion of the ECFMG.'

Suppressing anger and adding polish to my native tongue, I replied: 'Well, I am pleased the IDPR recognizes I can speak English, - when given the chance.'

At that time, I overlooked the significance of passing the English test within ECFMG. I promptly exited and headed to O'Hare airport. Waiting for the return flight to the UK, my mind flashed back to 1975. Soon after completing our final MB, BS exams to qualify as doctors, a group of us medical students from King's decided to sit the ECFMG. We took advantage while the reams of knowledge remained in our memories. None of us considered practicing long-term in America; however, then, certification by ECFMG opened doors to training in America at mid-level (Fellowship, similar to SHO/Registrar) as a future option.

Given my prior experiences in the US as a medical student in New York (1971) and Boston (1974), I toyed with completing some post-graduate training in the USA. In 1975, the ECFMG offered the English test as optional. For fun, I decided to take that additional option having experienced the diverse use of language on both sides of the Atlantic. I passed easily knowing diaper meant nappy, sidewalk meant pavement, and so on, having been raised by a Canadian mother. Several friends balked at taking the English test option. Some took offence: 'What audacity. No need. We speak Her Majesty's tongue!'

On route to the Chicago airport, 'the penny dropped.' Without the English test, the ECFMG certification expires after ten years. I passed the ECFMG and accompanying English test 21 years before. Without the English test, to grant a license, the IDPR required completion in the USA of a three-year junior post (Fellowship) and American speciality Board examination in internal medicine and gastroenterology - a bridge too far. Be grateful for little mercies. More importantly, be thankful for planning ahead – decades ahead.

Back in Scotland, no details came regarding content and timing of the SPEX – the Special Purpose Examination. The IDPR denied appeals. After several transatlantic telephone calls, I learned the IDPR recently instigated this exam to screen specialists like me with careers long-established before 1988 and, therefore, exempt from taking 'The Boards' – to demonstrate proficiency in internal medicine and, in my case, also gastroenterology. Once more I needed to prove my capabilities by sitting a multiple-choice examination in general medicine at Fellowship (SHO/Registrar) level as if this were 1977-1978. The IDPR offered no advice on revision materials: 'The SPEX is new and untested.'

Back in Glasgow, in-between laboratory experiments, I became a student one more time, now facing my 46th birthday. I filled the dormitory room with classical medical textbooks on subjects I pored over more than two decades earlier to prepare for the MRCP Parts I and II. Thank goodness for long-term memory and extra training above and below the diaphragm. The main causes of heart failure are....... A first assessment of pulmonary hypertension involves.............

On a cold, sunny day in October 1996, having turned 46 years of age the month before, I took what I determined would be my last medicine proficiency exam. From Chicago O'Hare airport, I rode the 'EL' ('elevated' train which becomes a subway) to downtown Chicago and entered a nondescript skyscraper on Wacker Drive near the main shopping area, Michigan Avenue. At first, I assumed I entered the wrong building. Clerks and administrative staff moved effortlessly around offices. One pointed to a cubicle with a computer screen and electronic mouse. A small card gave simple instructions: 'Questions are timed. Press the button to start the timer. No need to sign out.' No other examinee entered in the building.

'Complications of ectopic pregnancy include all of the following except......'

'The first line medication to treat bipolar disorders is....'

After 25 questions on gynaecological conditions and more on psychiatry, the solitary question on hepatology offered incomplete choices. As with the 11-plus examination more than three decades earlier, I came away not knowing whether I passed or failed (Chapter 1. 'So, you want to be a doctor?'). For both examinations, the stakes were high. In 1963, without a pass at the 11-Plus exam, the journey to becoming a doctor would have ended before my 13th birthday based on my substandard primary education and lack of access to the A level curriculum required for medical school. Thirty-three years later, in 1996, I needed an American medical license to continue to practise as a doctor and, importantly, start a new chapter in life. Back to the airport, I returned to Scotland to await once more an exam result that would dictate my future.

I marvelled at passing the SPEX. Weeks later, a letter requested I return to Chicago to collect the medical license approval. Once again, I booked a one-way ticket. Without ceremony, the receptionist at IDPR handed me the approval letter to apply for an Illinois license (036). I left the office within minutes of arrival.

In a nearby café, I collected myself. *Deep breaths.* Thoughts of my reaction to the A-level results and acceptance into medical school, King's College London, 27 years ago: 'I have made it......I have made it.' This time there was no 'we'. Mother and Mary in New Zealand slept as I celebrated alone.

In Chicago, initially, I remained content borrowing laboratory space from other researchers without strings attached. Time passed writing grants, chapters in books and presenting at medical conferences. Caring for patients with complex liver diseases, including acute liver failure, brought me back to the clinical work left five years before. Slowly I overcame the hard landing of being in a new country, in a state known for weeks of freezing temperatures and without my supporting circle of longstanding friends in the UK. I began to feel accepted for my contribution despite the emotional baggage of recent struggles. For the first time in five years, I celebrated Christmas without worrying how to cover a mortgage.

Three years later, I met David, the love of my life, and moved to Texas in 2000 to marry and start a second career. Texas, along with many other states has a shortage of hepatologists, especially those with experience in critical care (liver transplantation, acute liver failure). Armed with an invitation letter to work in an institute for liver transplantation in San Antonio, I happily packed my bags and said goodbye to Chicago. No more cold winters. Would this change of plans be the last time? The United States, in many ways is not united. Each state has separate rules and regulations on diverse issues from an acceptable level of blood alcohol when driving to reciprocity or not for accepting medical training and licensing among the fifty states.

In 2000, Illinois and Texas shared no reciprocity on medical licensing. The Texas Medical Regulatory Board refused to recognize my full ('036') and unrestricted Illinois license to practice medicine and surgery. Moreover, the Texas Board disregarded five years of work in the USA as a senior attending (consultant) physician, a full professorship in a prestigious medical institution and invitation to work in a field (liver transplantation) with known acute shortages of specialists. I remembered that surgeon at Cook County facing the IDPR. The Texas State Board of Medical Examiners Board (akin to the IDPR) recognised the ECFMG certification; however, before obtaining a 036 license for Texas, they requested I return to medical school, albeit on an accelerated trajectory to graduate as a doctor - again. Any appeal to their decision would take more than 18 months due to a backlog of cases under review. Despite being acknowledged as an expert in liver disease, prior work in Illinois, a recently publishing a book in the US and UK on viral hepatitis and holding an E11 visa with a green card, these recognitions carried no sway.

Time to move on at age 50 and gladly so. Unlike fighting for many months to recognise my contribution to a research project (Chapter 15. 'Winning the battle, losing the war') my priorities changed. By now, I learned to let go, look forward and keep options open. Moreover, I prioritised my own happiness and well-being without guilt or regrets. After all, I had overcome many odds and achieved ends. Buoyed by a new life and happy, stable home, I applied to work as a physician in biotechnology drug development in a small company in Houston, Texas. Academic friends cast bets I would not last three months in the cutthroat, for-profit atmosphere of the business world, albeit in the non-commercial side of drug development and medical affairs. I focused on seeking approval of medications for Orphan Diseases – those uncommon conditions with no prior approved therapies. Repeatedly, I have been drawn to the unusual, the exceptions to the rule.

After leaving Chicago, I never looked back. Twenty years, and five biotechnology companies later, found me working in Texas, Australia and California, this time with moral support of my husband and our respective relatives and friends. Over decades as a physician-scientist I took part in overseeing the conduct of clinical trials. Along with many academic colleagues, I bemoaned the high cost of drugs. Naïvely I believed I understood biotechnology drug development. Not so. Once more, I became a student after I crossed from clinical academic medicine to the 'dark side' of for-profit business. Biotechnology development is high-risk. Many biotechnology companies and products fail despite all good intentions. Bringing a drug or medical device beyond regulatory approval and to market remains an outstanding and unlikely achievement. Failure is more likely than success. Progress, if any, is accomplished only after years, if not decades, of painstaking, multi-stage development and hundreds of millions of pounds in investment. Many workers in biotechnology never savour the success of witnessing approval by regulatory authorities and the market launch of a new drug or medical device. Within 12 years of working in biotechnology drug development, I experienced unusual success. I oversaw pivotal clinical trials and the approval of not one, but two, medications in separate companies and their respective launches to market; one for hepatitis B, one for idiopathic pulmonary fibrosis. These products have impacted the lives of millions of patients around the world.

Universities play a crucial role in biotechnology and often are the birthplace of scientific, medical and technological advances. Unfortunately, these most hallowed institutions typically do not have the infrastructure or financial resources to develop a drug, device or research project beyond the early stages. Small and medium-sized biotechnology companies often form the incubators for many early-stage products and projects that require baby steps in development. Equally they hold the graveyard for many products that fail to progress beyond infancy due to safety concerns or lack of efficacy. Accordingly, small- and medium-sized companies typically bear the brunt of the risk in product development. The odds of success are low. The rewards are high. The cost of bringing a drug to market often exceeds one billion US dollars if prior failures are included. In contrast, many large biotechnology and pharmaceutical companies are relatively risk-averse and prefer to acquire projects and products from universities and smaller companies only in the later stages of development when the chances of success rise. A few companies with deep financial pockets will acquire a project or product to 'kill the competition.' Regardless, early, and late-stage, product and project development in medicine remains a costly enterprise whether successful or not.

I enjoyed the fast-paced, risk-taking, atmosphere of the small companies, no doubt a reflection of the years I spent in the high-risk environment of critical care hepatology. Colleagues in academia showed surprise at my newly found enthusiasm for working in biotechnology. Was there any conflict of interest given my life-long resolve to put patients first? Fortunately, the companies that employed me upheld strict codes of conduct separating medical (non-commercial) from commercial aspects of the work. These companies restricted communication between staff in medical affairs and sales personnel. We had separate buildings, dining and recreation, areas. The integrity of such companies depends on a visible firewall between these two sides of the business.

I view the clinical practice of medicine as a life-long apprenticeship. Medicine is one of the few professions where longevity becomes an asset. Many physicians join biotechnology and pharmaceutical companies soon after qualifying as doctors. They have the medical knowledge but, understandably, lack the practical experience that comes with a quarter of a century 'in the field'. Thus, I became the 'go-to' person for complex medical matters arising with subjects (patients) participating in clinical trials. Although known as the 'happy hepatologist,' I comfortably discussed medical issues with executives, outside key opinion leaders (KOLs) and regulatory authorities in the USA, Canada and UK relating to drug development for peanut allergy, heart failure, HIV infection, pulmonary hypertension, pulmonary fibrosis and more. Also, staff called on me when an employee became ill or required medical advice on site. Word spread 'the doctor is in the house.'

In 2015 after completing a successful clinical trial and filing for regulatory approval of pirfenidone for idiopathic pulmonary fibrosis (IPF), the company (InterMune) merged with Genentech/Roche. Time to move on. I arrived financially and emotionally to a safe harbour. I chartered my own course to become an independent advisor, consultant and board member to the biotech/pharma/Artificial Intelligence industry. My husband David and I settled in Texas. We live comfortably and peacefully on Galveston, a small island, and within a ten-minute walk to the Gulf of Mexico. Those who know the winding path of my story agree 'I have made it' (Chapter 7. 'With gratitude to teachers and strangers').

Not so for mother. During her final 12 years, then in New Zealand, she struggled to integrate into the local community, a situation worsened by failing vision and the frailty of old age. My sister, Mary, a community nurse, provided mother with a home of her own and cared for her as a patient. Mother died there in 2006 a bitter woman, resentful over her lot in life and ashamed of being a divorcée.

In contrast, father moved on, remarried and embraced his role as 'beloved grandpa' to Mary's two children (my nieces). My sister and I felt the void of never knowing our grandparents and being estranged from other relatives. Mary made the decision to keep her own family in contact with father through the years. My nieces became aware of our unhappy upbringing, their grandparents acrimonious divorce and grandma's limited circumstances. However, Mary and I agreed not to reveal to them the details of grandpa's past behaviour especially towards grandmother and me. Consequently, for some time I became the outsider once more – this time to the inner circle of remaining family. With resolve to attend the wedding of my older niece, I met father after a gap of 38 years to demonstrate there would be no disruption on my niece's special day. Father walked his granddaughter down the aisle in place of her late father. Subsequently, father and I communicated infrequently albeit cordially. I learned through family that over the years he followed my career through the newspapers, television, radio and other public appearances. In the few times we met and corresponded he never acknowledged or expressed to me any pride in my achievements. Moreover, he showed no remorse for his prior actions – after all, 'You [I] did all right in the end.' I gave no response. He died in 2013.

Chapter 17: Didn't we do well?!

The tourist bus rounded the corner between North Parade Road and Pulteney Street in Bath, a Roman city in England, a hundred miles west of London. This small city situated on the river Avon, is unique in many ways and features prominently as a 'must see' in travel guides for the West of England. The city is listed as a World Heritage site for its architecture among other attractions.

That day in May 2004 brought glorious sunshine. My husband, David, and I sat among other sightseers on the top deck of an open double-decker bus. The guide, a young man, came bounding up the stairs:

'As you will see, on your right is a building built in unusual Victorian Gothic style by Elkington Gill, a local architect, dating from around 1858. This is the Magistrate's Court. Decades ago, this building was a convent and school, the name I do not recall, a French convent high school for girls that closed down....'

He paused about to describe another tourist highlight when David interrupted him: 'My wife here was head girl at that school, La Sainte Union Convent.'

The guide wanted more information but kept to his tour script as other notable sites passed by. 'We are now crossing the river Avon. This river used to flood almost every year....'

We smiled at the irony of much water passing under the bridge of my life since 1969, the year I finished at that former high school. By 2004, I had lived in the USA 10 years and we had been married three. David knew my history in puzzle pieces but we both sought to complete the picture by putting the jigsaw together. Over the years, David and several others encouraged me to write my story.

We planned our journey to the UK in 2004 for three main reasons. First, I wanted to show David my high school (years 9-14) at La Sainte Union Convent. There my journey began (1963-1969) as I worked up from the bottom of the bottom class at age 13 to becoming head girl in my final, and extra, year at school.

Second, I wanted David to see King's College London (KCL). I am a King's graduate through and through. All five degrees awarded through the University of London were taken under KCL's' umbrella. These span twenty years (1969-1989) and include a Masters in Immunology from Chelsea College (1980-1982), soon to merge with KCL in 1985. King's College Hospital (KCH) and medical school are home to me too, having spent there my formative undergraduate (1972-1975), and postgraduate (1976; 1983-1991), clinical years.

At King's I found my wings. There I learned to ask for help to rise above the clouds. My generation rode the cusp of change as opportunities began to open for women to advance in science and medicine, but not quite yet. As one of few women in medical school in the late 1960s, I had to find my voice. The respect and trust of peers and superiors came slowly. Gender equality required further effort within the male-dominated specialities of gastroenterology and hepatology.

KCL in 2004 had changed from 1969, including the Strand, a 'Brutalist-style', building completed during my undergraduate years (1969-1972). When new, architects considered this concrete structure 'modern,' 'bold' and 'interesting' - as with the Barbican Centre, constructed in the same era and style. Thirty-five years later, my views aged along with the Strand building. The grey façade shows the worse for wear and is out of style with the surrounding architecture. Gone is the abstract sculpture behind and adjacent to the entrance to the Grade I listed building. Reggie, the lion mascot, continues to hold court in the main foyer. His presence and image were on full display as students from KCL and nearby LSE marched along the Strand to protest the Vietnam war and 'ban the bomb' when I was a first year (freshman) student (1969-1970).

Inside KCL, some lecture rooms on the ground floor have been remodelled into cafeterias and places for students to gather. No such facilities in my time. A floor or two above, the dissection room is repurposed with desks and computers, leaving only the white wall tiles, now faded, as a reminder of its original use. The smell of formaldehyde is long gone except in my memory. The nearby main lecture theatre for preclinical students is conserved as a historical reminder of my generation, including names etched into the tiered wooden benches. All rooms look small but were large in my recollection. In 1971, the Physiology Department and laboratory occupied the top floor of the main building with magnificent views of the Thames and Southbank. We BSc students witnessed the building of the Southbank Theatre complex. Physics, and engineering, students were less fortunate with their departments located in the basements. Worse, vermin invaded their facilities when the Thames flooded, a not-infrequent occurrence during my time. Ratcatchers earned a handsome living according to the tides.

The chapel, a centre-piece of the Strand campus, is lovingly restored. I recall organ music sounding throughout the building especially during ceremonies for ordinands. I would have one ear attuned to the music as the other tuned in to lectures on medical ethics as part of the AKC course.

Glass panelled bookcases line some of the corridors outside the chapel. During our visit in 2004, among the bookcases, I spotted a non-descript grey radiograph film with black dots in ever-decreasing circles.

'Ah, Rosalind Franklin – one of her crystallography films – remember "radiograph 51!"'

In 1969, Maurice Wilkins (Nobel Prize for Medicine or Physiology 1962, shared with Watson and Crick) gave one indecipherable lecture on the structure of DNA to us freshmen students. What an irony that Nobel prize authorities denied Dr Franklin, not once, but twice, from sharing such recognition due to her untimely death in 1958. Her additional work on the crystalline structure of viral proteins and nucleic acids is a seminal contribution to science for which her superior, Aaron Klug, received the Nobel prize in Chemistry in 1982. Although recognition of the contribution of researchers in science and medicine has improved, more transparency is needed. Structural and social racism and other inequalities also need to be addressed within these hallowed disciplines.

Third, and finally, we came to attend a ceremony at the Royal College of Physicians (RCP) in central London where I would be inducted as a Fellow (FRCP). Two years earlier, I became a Fellow of the American College of Physicians (FACP). These Fellowships are prestigious. In the UK, the nominee is a recognised specialist typically with three or more years as a consultant in the UK or at least ten years at comparable level (e.g., Attending in the USA) if an international candidate. Only Members of the Royal College of Physicians (MRCP) are eligible for this higher accolade. Only a holder of FRCP can nominate another. My nomination came by no less than the President of the Royal College of Physicians (PRCP) with assignation into a specific (second) category of exceptional persons, the first category being for Nobel prize winners and other celebrated dignitaries. A third category of members may be automatically listed for consideration but typically after many years as a specialist and associate specialist (SAS). Regardless, all categories acknowledge persons with exceptional knowledge, expertise and experience in their chosen field.

We lodged near the Royal College of Physicians. The College overlooks Regent's Park, one of eight Royal Parks in the city centre and among the most beautiful in central London. We took a brief walk around the rose garden – to smell the roses of life - before crossing the narrow street to enter the College.

A young doctor bounded up to me in the hallway, all smiles. He shook my hand vigorously:

'Oh, I recognise you, Dr Fagan! You taught me liver disease. I still do liver biopsy your way!'

We laughed as my husband looked on, puzzled by our humorous exchange over a procedure involving a long needle and sharp blade. I let him into a long-held secret: 'There must be more than 50 doctors I taught liver biopsy using the needle in the left-hand, despite their being right-handed.' I am dominantly left-handed.

As we walked further through the foyer, the Vice President (VP) of the Royal College of Physicians, Robert Pointer, cornered me. He looked agitated. Our paths last crossed a decade before in less auspicious circumstances (Chapter 15. 'Winning the battle, losing the war'). In 1995, the Royal Free Hospital School of Medicine appointed him as my counsellor following an internal tribunal that contested any claim I had to my research. Professor Pointer had offered no solution to the loss of my research, grant funding and appointment within his department after my project had been sold off to a US pharmaceutical company. 'The future is up to you,' he counselled.

Professor Pointer seemed uncomfortable in our presence with sheaves of papers in disarray as he located my name on the list – a good excuse to avoid looking me straight in the eye: 'Ah, hmm, Fagan, how should I address you – professor or doctor?'

'Doctor is fine. I live in America now where even Nobel Prize winners in medicine are called doctor.'

He continued to fumble with his papers: 'So, I need to make sure I have all your titles and achievements listed correctly.... professor of internal medicine...oh, and paediatrics...and senior consultant in Chicago......Fellow of the Royal College of Pathologists.......'

'Please include that I am an FACP - Fellow of the American College of Physicians too.'

He paused: 'Ah, yes, I have that down here somewhere.'

More fumbling: 'You are being inducted in category two (II) for your contributions to research in molecular virology and medicine....... and the list goes on.' He wanted to move on. With a nod, he promptly left.

David knew about my prior interactions with Professor Pointer in 1994-1995. We mused at the irony that a Royal College appointed him, above many, to announce in public my accolades when a decade before he and the Royal Free Hospital School of Medicine considered me a persona non grata (Chapter 15. 'Winning the battle, losing the war').

The ceremony went smoothly. After induction of external dignitaries (category I), an officer of the Royal College announced category II. I looked around but did not recognise any of the few 'Fellows' in my category. We shook hands with a line of College officers as Robert Pointer, in his role as VP of the Royal College, read out each nominee's titles and achievements. Swept up in the moment, the paradox hit me further only after acknowledging the handshakes and congratulations. As I moved down the line, another officer of the Royal College stepped forward. I identified her as a panel member of that fated tribunal at the Royal Free Hospital School of Medicine in 1995. Now all smiles: 'Well done. Don't forget to shake hands with all of us. Congratulations.'

Keep calm and carry on. Now I could move on.

After the ceremony I reunited with David who watched from the upstairs gallery overlooking the proceedings. In the toasting room, Professor Pointer approached once more, this time smiling and looking more relaxed than before: 'Well, I always knew you would do well. I am glad you took my recommendation to go to America.'

Lost for words, the look of astonishment on my face spoke volumes. He scurried off to confront another inductee.

In need of fresh air, David and I walked outside into the adjoining garden. May is a beautiful month in the UK for nature to reveal itself as on this picture-perfect day. Roses and other flowers in full bloom in the College Garden did not disappoint. We reflected on the many twists and turns in my life that culminated in this special day.

Around 50 people mingled amid tables of champagne and hors d'oeuvres. An inductee approached us from behind as the toastmaster raised his glass to honour the newly minted FRCPs:

'To the new Fellows.'

We raised our glasses.

Only then did I turn to acknowledge the inductee beside us. Of course, there she was, instantly recognisable - Jocelyn Corrigan, the head girl at my high school two years ahead of me. In high school, Jocelyn crushed my spirit on learning of my life-long resolution to become a doctor with her admonition: "You can't read medicine. You're working class." (Chapter 1. 'So, you want to become a doctor?'). She turned to face me, as elegant, poised and eloquent as I remembered her over four decades before. This time she remarked with a smile: 'Didn't we do well?!'

This time, no tears. I smiled back: 'Oh yes indeed. I agree.'

Epilogue

The puzzle pieces of my life's journey began to fit together once I passed the half century mark. There are observations and lessons to pass on to others who find themselves an outsider. Twists and turns along the way mould the person. When young, I yearned to fit in with peers. Instead, as an outsider, from an undereducated and different ('odd') background, I channeled my energies to reach a life-long goal that many deemed unreachable - to become a doctor.

The discipline and survival skills learned as an army brat, attending multiple schools in different countries, made me a citizen of the world. Admittedly, I pause when answering the question:

'Where do you come from?'

'Do you mean where I was born, where I live now, or where I belong?'

I am comfortable being among people whose first language is not English. In common with my husband, David, an American born and raised in Argentina, we have lived and worked in more than one country and settled in one different from that of our births.

Timing can be everything. In 2007, I became an American citizen. Unlike my unfortunate mother, compelled to forsake irrevocably her citizenship by birth, I retain mine – the best of two worlds.

Some traits are hard to dismiss. The unhappy family life as a child makes me appreciative of a safe, stable and happy home. Deep down, the insecurity of once being homeless and penniless remains despite not being 'out on the street' due to the kindness of nuns who provided shelter. I am frugal and take nothing for granted. No act of kindness, however small, goes unnoticed. My firm belief that education is key to unlocking the door to opportunity reflects how close I came to missing out. How mother missed out. How father failed to appreciate the opportunities afforded by education.

Mother's hard work and my arduous study at high school bore fruit as I worked my way up from the bottom of the bottom to the top of the top class and became head girl.

My generation, born shortly after World War II, rode the cusp of change as opportunities began to open for women in science and medicine, but not quite yet. Women were in the minority in medical school in the 1960s-1970s. Even fewer carried my pedigree – poorly educated until a teenager and from a lower working-class, dysfunctional, military family.

Gaining a place in medical school at King's College, London was a conquest. I had arrived; however, future mountains rose to conquer. As a medical student I experienced discrimination as a woman and one from a working-class background. As a doctor, I faced my own serious ill-health that took decades to solve and resolve. I had to heal myself.

I learned, albeit slowly, to find my voice. Speaking up for myself earned the respect and trust of peers and superiors.

Over the years, interviewers for work, supervisors and other contacts invariably comment on a pattern in my career of journeying down less travelled roads with resolve to achieve ends, and then some. They point to my resolve in overcoming the odds stacked against me – a dysfunctional home and inadequate education in childhood, entering medicine and choosing a male-dominated speciality when few women were accepted, and while overcoming a major illness. The student summer internship at Albert Einstein, New York (1971) piques their interest and curiosity while silently noting my gender and likely religious preference based on family name: 'So, tell us how (on earth) you managed to obtain an internship at "Einstein".' (Chapter 8. 'King's College, London (1969-1972); medical school, firsts'). As for my career path, I not only survived working on the Liver Unit at King's but flourished. Few women in my era chose hepatology, a demanding and underrecognised speciality. Despite an early commitment to hepatology, the resolve to aim for top junior posts in chest medicine and cardiology at a precarious time in my career (Chapters 11-13) predictably raises eyebrows. These diversions continue to pay dividends decades later after I branched out beyond 'liver' into biotechnology and drug development.

To all these queries about my 'odd' choices and aiming high, my response remains the same: 'I had nothing to lose.'

Resolve and being an outsider can bring dividends; however, be prepared to wait for resolution and aim to navigate roadblocks. I learned to accept being 'odd' and later wore that moniker with pride long after achieving ends - my childhood aspirations to qualify in medicine. As a junior doctor starting out, I benefitted from working in – and surviving - the renowned Liver Unit at King's. That trial by fire successively opened doors to other 'A'-listed departments and institutions. In return, those elite institutions gained a reliable and dedicated workhorse who kept her head down and never missed a day off work. However, once I came within reach of senior status (Senior Lecturer, Consultant) and challenged my rights, some supervisors branded me as difficult, demanding, ungrateful. Doors in the UK closed to further advancement despite being 'overqualified.' Medicine, especially in academia, is practiced within a tightly knit community.

Regardless of these challenges, within hepatology I found a professional home. Recognition as a 'card-carrying' hepatologist took more than a decade in the speciality not recognised as separate from gastroenterology in my era. Treatment options for patients with liver disease were few when I embarked on my chosen career. I, an outsider, cared for outsiders. I started in hepatology when the field began to expand and embrace advances in science and technology. Over decades I witnessed remarkable achievements from laboratory bench to the bedside of clinical medicine. I cared for the first adult and paediatric liver transplant recipients in the UK. My world tour in 1988 to promote the value of vaccination against hepatitis B placed me on the world stage. Invitations followed to lecture around the world, write a book on viral hepatitis for the UK and USA and contribute to seminal reference medical texts.

Mother's continued labour to see me enter medical school and my unwavering resolve to become and remain a physician–scientist paid further dividends, but at a high cost to both of us. Mother fared poorly. Fully aware of her lack of education, she resigned herself to menial work as a cleaner, joining the millions of essential, but faceless, workers. Mother remained separated from her own relatives. Canada, her birth country, denied reinstatement of citizenship. She carried her generation's stigma of being a divorcée to her grave.

My price was loneliness and self-imposed isolation, as I battled in secret poor health and in public the prejudice against women, all to overcome the odds and retain a foothold on the steep ladder of academic medicine. I paid the price gladly only because I survived and surpassed my singularly focused end goal in life to qualify in medicine. The challenges in high school, during medical training and beyond were overcome through the support and encouragement of friends and strangers. Teachers too played a key role, giving me the benefit of the doubt. They saw my potential rather than the inherited disadvantages.

My story also chronicles a journey of living and coping with uncertainty. Serious illness overshadowing teenage years and medical training threatened a hard-won career. Determination and resolve led to a self-diagnosis when such conditions were poorly understood. Those who supported me became friends for life. I rode another wave, this one as a patient with timely new treatments, and never looked back. A resolute focus - 'keep your eye on the prize' - allowed me to adapt and start over several times in my career and life.

When circumstances beyond my control thwarted years of research as a physician-scientist, resolve and perseverance were taxed. By then, I learned my limits and belatedly overcame a lifetime hesitancy to ask for help. Friends became family once more with their unwavering support since my relatives were located half a world away.

In retrospect, my personal choice to 'go it alone', when faced with hardship and uncertainty, likely would have been eased by reaching out more for help. Do not let pride or embarrassment inhibit asking for support. I encourage students to seek a mentor and coach early on in their personal, and professional, lives and before facing hardship. Mentors and coaches find reward in seeing others succeed – a win-win situation.

In the end, having found my feet and voice, I took a positive step to change the trajectory of my life. At forty-four years of age, I emigrated to America to start over again. Two years later, I took my last proficiency examination in general medicine. I married for the first time at fifty years of age and changed careers from full-time medicine to biotechnology drug and medical device development. Belatedly, I closed the door to my thwarted research and looked forward to beginning a new chapter in a different profession (biotechnology) outside the familiar realm of academia. I could envisage a happier and more fulfilling life for myself, now with a supportive husband.

Several important people in my life (father, former Vice Dean at KCH, 'counsellor' at RFHSM and a head girl at high school) acknowledged I did well - in the end. However, this belated recognition seemed to absolve each from admitting to their former adversarial behaviour. None apologised. I could have shunned or admonished them. Instead, I resolved to 'keep calm and carry on' to preserve the inner harmony I later learned to nurture in my life. I recommend readers follow the wise maxim: 'Do not wait for someone to bring you flowers. Plant your own garden and decorate your own soul.' (Luther Burbank, horticulturalist).

I encourage readers to keep one eye looking forward and plan to walk towards a better career, and life, rather than away from a negative situation.

Take heed. There are advantages to being an outsider. There is room for all of us. We should treasure our exceptions.

As for my career, I straddle two worlds – those of medicine and biotechnology. In overseeing successful clinical trials, the launch of new drugs, and being an adviser to medical industry, I continue to impact patients -- especially those underserved. The improbable aspirations of a four-year old are more than satisfied.

All I ever wanted was to be a doctor.

About the author

Elizabeth Fagan is a transatlantic physician, academic hepatologist, gastroenterologist and biotechnology executive. Elizabeth and her sister, Mary, were born in the UK; however, as children of army parents, the family lived abroad in several countries including Singapore and Cyprus. They returned finally to the UK when Elizabeth was 12 years old. She completed her high school (years 9-14) at La Sainte Union Convent grammar school in Bath, Avon (now Somerset) where she became head girl.

Her undergraduate (BSc physiology with first class honours and MB, BS in medicine and surgery), and post-graduate degrees (MSc with distinction in immunology and MD degree in molecular virology) are from the University of London, King's College. She is a proud Associate of King's College (AKC).

Elizabeth received her post-graduate medical training in adult and paediatric hepatology (liver disease) and gastroenterology at King's College Hospital and Hammersmith Hospital (Royal Postgraduate Medical School) in London, UK. Additional junior medical posts were on the professorial units at Royal Brompton (respiratory disease) and London Chest Hospitals (cardiology). She spent four years as a Senior Wellcome Research Fellow at the Royal Free Hospital School of Medicine, London University working full-time on the molecular virology of acute liver failure.

Elizabeth came to the USA in 1994 and became a naturalised American citizen in 2007. She holds a medical license in Illinois, USA. In Chicago she is a professor (now adjunct) of internal medicine and pediatrics at Rush Presbyterian, St. Luke's Medical Center, specializing in liver disease.

Elizabeth also has extensive experience in biotechnology drug and medical device development having worked full-time for biotechnology companies in Texas, California and Australia. She sits on the board of directors for a UK-based biotechnology company.

She has been honoured as a Fellow of the Royal College of Pathologists, Royal College of Physicians and American College of Physicians. Elizabeth has published over 100 scientific papers and 30 book chapters on liver disease and a book in the UK and USA on viral hepatitis. She is a public speaker and has lectured around the world on health issues including viral hepatitis and vaccination.

Elizabeth lives with her husband, David Smith, and two cats in Galveston, Texas.

Elizabeth supports a student for six years on the King's College London Extended Medical Degree Programme (EMDP) through the Elizabeth A. Fagan Bursary. The EMDP is designed for students studying A-levels or Access to Medicine at a non-selective state school in the UK. The course offers a more graduated introduction to medical study than the standard MBBS degree and provides significant academic and pastoral support.

The bursary award is based on financial circumstances. More information on the EMDP is available: *Extended Medical Degree Programme - King's College London (kcl.ac.uk).*

78004775R00098